MW01231364

To Mary,
Whose passion for Truth is
an example for all. Thank you.
Annette M Fauci, O.C.D.S

THE GUIDE TO
Christian Success

Annette M. Fauci, O.C.D.S.

PONTIFF PUBLISHING COMPANY

CONYERS, GEORGIA

Print ISBN: 978-1-54390-712-4

eBook ISBN: 978-1-54390-713-1

Cover Design by Suzanne Fauci

Praise and thanksgiving to the Holy Trinity, One God,

the Father, the Son, and the Holy Spirit,

and many thanks to Charles and Jeanette.

TABLE OF CONTENTS

INTRODUCTION IX

CHAPTER 1 *Prophets - To Tell the Truth!* 1

How Do We Know Who Is Telling the Truth? 3

False Prophets 4

The Good Pastor 8

The Wannabees.. 10

Are You Ready for the Challenge? 10

...And the Reward?.. 11

What Christians Do.. 11

Socialism/Communism Is Not Christian................................12

Take the First Step 13

CHAPTER 2 *Why is it so Difficult?*....................................14

Free Will 101..16

Choices 18

CHAPTER 3 *Who is Jesus?*..19

"In the beginning"..20

Lost by Disobedience...By Obedience Won............................20

The God-Man Foretold 25

Jesus Is Truly God... 28

...and Jesus Is Truly Man 30

CHAPTER 4 *Jesus Proclaims the Kingdom of God* 33

Where Do We Start?.. 34

Jesus as Brother, Friend 36

World at War 37

Propaganda 38

God's Abundant Communication..40

It's Time for a Story..44

CHAPTER 5 *Lord, Teach Us to Pray*.. 47

Why Did Jesus, Who Is God and Man, Pray? 47

The Prayer Jesus Taught Us 49

CHAPTER 6 *The Beatitudes* 56

"Blessed are the poor in spirit, for theirs is the kingdom of heaven." 58

The Beatitudes Are One Instruction.. 60

"Blessed are those who mourn, for they will be comforted." 60

"Blessed are the meek, for they will inherit the earth." 61

"Blessed are those who hunger and thirst for righteousness" 62

"Blessed are the merciful, for they will receive mercy."............................. 63

"Blessed are the pure in heart, for they will see God." 64

"Blessed are the peacemakers, for they will be called children of God."......... 64

"Blessed are those who are persecuted for righteousness' sake for theirs is the kingdom of heaven." 66

"Blessed are you when people revile you and persecute you and utter all kinds of evil against you falsely on my account." 67

CHAPTER 7 *The Ten Commandments* 69

The Great Corruption 70

How to Love God 73

How to Love Your Neighbor 77

CHAPTER 8 *The Grace of Church*... 104

Jesus Established His Church 104

Apostolic Succession 107

The Grace of Holy Priesthood.. 111

The Grace of Baptism 113

The Grace of Confirmation... 115

The Grace of Certainty That We Are Forgiven 117

The Grace of the Breaking of the Bread 119

The Grace of Healing 121

The Grace of Marriage 121

The Holy Temple 124

CHAPTER 9 *Christianity as Enigma* 125

Good vs. Evil as Enigma 125

God's Justice Is Enigma 133

Death is Enigma 135

The Holy Trinity Is Enigma 137

CHAPTER 10 *Suffering with Jesus* 139

See His Love for You! 139

Share His Love for You! 140

Loving Jesus 143

CHAPTER 11 *The Cross is the Sum of All Wisdom and Knowledge* 146

The Cross Exposes "the Inner Thoughts of Many" 146

The Lessons Taught by the Cross 147

CHAPTER 12 *Journey to Union* 153

Our Prophetic Calling 155

Biblical Prophecy Fulfilled 158

Biblical Prophecy Yet to Be Fulfilled 160

The End of the Ages 168

CHAPTER 13 *Blessed Are Those Who Follow the Lamb* 170

The Seven Churches 171

The Seven Seals 175

The Seven Trumpets 177

The Seven Bowls 183

The End of Babylon 185

The Justice of God 187

END NOTES 191

BIBLIOGRAPHY 198

INTRODUCTION

*B*y the grace of the Holy Spirit, I have endeavored to write down simply and clearly the Gospel message that Jesus wants us to live in these last days. If you were baking cookies and had replaced the sugar with salt in error, wouldn't you want to discover the mistake before you bit into that first bad cookie? So it is with this book. It is meant to expose the bad batches of dough in our lives so we can toss them out and start fresh.

We start on a journey when our lives begin. Our intended destination is heaven, but the instructions are no longer clear. The message of the Gospel has been complicated and confused by worldly pressures and shepherds who pasture themselves, leading God's children down blind alleys into darkness.

God's commandments, his words of love, have been corrupted to serve a culture of power and greed. Now, as in all of history, humankind still thinks that power belongs to those with the most money. It is a shame we have not learned that true power comes from God and is given to those with the most love, those who love God with all their hearts and who love their neighbors as themselves. This guide is intended to refocus us on what Scripture says God deems important as we prepare for the next phase of life: eternity.

CHAPTER 1

Prophets - To Tell the Truth!

What is a prophet? Does it matter to us in this day and age? Aren't prophets extinct? Some people think prophecy means foretelling the future. Prophets are not fortune tellers! In the book of Revelation, after we meet the Four Horsemen of the Apocalypse, we are introduced to two prophets who call the world to repentance: "And I will grant my two witnesses authority to prophesy for one thousand two hundred and sixty days, wearing sackcloth" (Revelations 11:3). Would you recognize these prophets? What is a prophet?

> *"...This people honor me with their lips, but their hearts are far from me; in vain do they worship me, teaching human precepts as doctrines."*
> *Mark 7:6-7*

Peter the apostle defined *prophet* in his letter 2 Peter 1:20-21, "First of all you must understand this, that no prophecy of scripture is a matter of one's own interpretation, because no prophecy ever came by human will, but men and women moved by the Holy Spirit spoke from God." Peter further warns, "But false prophets also arose among the people, just as there will be false teachers among you, who will secretly bring in destructive opinions. They will even deny the Master who bought them–bringing swift destruction upon themselves. Even so, many will follow their licentious ways, and because of these teachers the way of truth will be maligned. And in their greed they will exploit you with deceptive words..." (2 Peter 2:1-3).

God deals firmly with false prophets in both the Old and New Testaments. One example is given in 2 Kings 5. Naaman, the King of Aram's pagan army commander, was afflicted with leprosy. His wife had a Jewish slave girl who told Naaman to seek out Elisha, the great Hebrew prophet. Elisha's cure? He simply instructed the powerful army commander to bathe in the Jordan River. Naaman was indignant. He had no intention of bathing in the muddy waters of the Jordan. Fortunately, cooler heads prevailed. Naaman's servants convinced him to do as Elisha had instructed and Naaman was healed. He returned to Elisha and offered him gifts in gratitude. Elisha refused the gifts and directed Naaman's gratitude toward God. As a result, Naaman promised to offer sacrifice only to the one, true God of Israel. However, Elisha's servant, Gehazi, got greedy. He found Naaman on the road to Aram and told him that Elisha had changed his mind and asked for one silver talent and two festal garments. Naaman generously offered two talents and servants to help Gehazi carry the gifts; gifts gratefully given in **payment** for the cure. Gehazi undid the point made by Elisha: The God of Israel is a living God who cares for himself and his children. Elisha wanted Naaman to understand that his healing was solely the work of the God of Israel. As punishment for his deception, and his greater crime of heresy, Gehazi was afflicted with leprosy.

In the New Testament, Elymas opposed the teachings of the apostle Paul and schemed to turn the Proconsul Sergius Paulus away from the faith. Paul, filled with the Holy Spirit, confronted Elymas and said, "...You son of the devil, you enemy of all righteousness, full of all deceit and villainy, will you not stop making crooked the straight paths of the Lord? And now listen–the hand of the Lord is against you, and you will be blind for a while, unable to see the sun." Immediately mist and darkness came over him, and he went about groping for someone to lead him by the hand" (Acts 13:10-11). Since Elymas was only temporarily blinded, we might think that God in his mercy used blindness to help Elymas see the truth.

The above false prophets, Gehazi and Elymas, were struck by God's immediate consequences for their self-serving deceptions. For other false prophets, the consequences are not as swift, but Peter warns: "…Their condemnation, pronounced against them long ago, has not been idle, and their destruction is not asleep" (2 Peter 2:3).

How Do We Know Who Is Telling the Truth?

How do we keep from being confused by false teachers, phony pastors, and fake prophets? After all, we begin as both physical and spiritual children. We learn from family, then Sunday school teachers and pastors. If those people are corrupt, or if their understanding of Scripture is confused, we are misled. It is disturbing that there are so many different Christian denominations (some 30,000 exist), and even more disturbing that they teach different "truths." Let this be clear. There is only one Truth: the Truth Jesus taught to his apostles; the Truth shared with us through his apostles; the Truth protected and safeguarded by loyal and valiant successors to the apostles from century to century to this day.

Jesus warns, "Beware of false prophets, who come to you in sheep's clothing but inwardly are ravenous wolves." (Matthew 7:15). Prophets, sharers of God's Word, have an obligation to lift up God's children, not to lift themselves up on the backs of God's children. There are too many false prophets, too much greed, too much feel-good scriptural interpretation, and too many divisions in Christianity!

False Prophets

How are we to know if our spiritual guides are misleading us? Simply, a holy pastor will lead as Jesus taught his apostles to lead. We must not accept spiritual guidance from anyone who offers less. Therefore:

Beware of pastors who proclaim themselves models of perfection. What arrogance! At the Last Supper, Jesus washed the feet of his disciples, a job usually reserved for the lowliest slaves, then told them, "For I have set you an example, that you also should do as I have done to you. Very truly, I tell you, servants are not greater than their master, nor are messengers greater than the one who sent them" (John 13:15-16). The truly loving, unselfish service of a humble pastor will hold him up as an example to his flock. Run away from perfect pastors before you find yourself following their example of false pride and exaggerated self-importance.

Beware of pastors who entertain rather than enlighten by the Word of God. Entertainment abounds while the Word of God is neglected. These charlatans offer entertainment to draw crowds and fatten collection plates. How shallow are those who flock to these pastors! A few words about God surrounded by razzle-dazzle and glitz and they believe they have worshipped God. Simon the Magician was like these worshipers. He followed Philip around Samaria amazed at the miracles he was performing. He could not see that Philip's miracles were actually performed by the power of the Holy Spirit at work in him. He only saw a man performing feats of magic.[1] The Word of God shared in the power of the Holy Spirit is splendor enough! These false prophets offer no more spiritual guidance than a sports announcer at a ball game and are to be avoided as a waste of time. At least you are not being spiritually misled by listening to the ball game!

Beware of pastors who ask to see proof of income to verify that you are tithing ten percent. Beware of pastors who charge a membership fee to join their churches. What's next? A credit report to make sure you can afford to attend their church? Tithes must be freely and lovingly given, not coerced. And a membership fee? The apostle Paul worked a second job so he would not be a burden to his spiritual community.[2] And what of God's children who cannot afford the membership fee? Are they to be denied access to Baptism and the Word of God? Such practices are anti-Christ! Jesus freely taught all who were willing to listen and he made his feelings about profiteering from the Word of God very clear while in the temple at Jerusalem.

First a little background on the temple—the Court of the Gentiles, the outermost court of the temple built by Herod the Great, was set up as a marketplace where foreign currency was exchanged and animals for sacrifices were purchased by temple worshipers from all over the world. In addition, under Mosaic Law, every male over the age of nineteen had to pay the temple tax. Only a specific coin, a Hebrew half-shekel, was accepted to pay the tax and purchase the sacrificial animals. Moneychangers sold these half-shekel coins to worshipers at a premium. This system was a real moneymaker.

"Then they came to Jerusalem. And he entered the temple and began to drive out those who were selling and those who were buying in the temple, and he overturned the tables of the money changers and the seats of those who sold doves; and he would not allow anyone to carry anything through the temple. He was teaching and saying, 'Is it not written, 'My house shall be called a house of prayer for all nations? But you have made it a den of robbers.'" And when the chief priests and the scribes heard it, they kept looking for a way to kill him; for they were afraid of him, because the whole crowd was spellbound by his teaching" (Mark 11:15-18). Jesus did not approve of using Mosaic Law to line the temple leaders' pockets! He warned, "The scribes and the Pharisees sit on Moses' seat; therefore, do whatever they teach you and follow it; but do not do as they do, for they do not practice what they teach. They tie up heavy burdens, hard to bear, and lay them on the shoulders of others; but they themselves are unwilling to lift a finger to move them" (Matthew 23:2-4). We are brothers and sisters in Christ. Churches should be managed like families, not as burdensome taxing organizations!

Beware of pastors who display their personal wealth as a sign of how blessed they are by God. Those who claim that their prosperity signifies God's approval of their ministry are deceiving the faithful! Such teachings are anti-Christ. They oppose what Jesus said about wealth. Wealth is *not* a badge of being blessed by God, but is a tool entrusted to people to be used to glorify God and help humankind, not to glorify and help themselves. After Jesus was baptized by John in the Jordan River, he spent forty days in the desert where he was tempted by the devil. "Then the devil led him up and showed him in an instant all the kingdoms of the world. And the devil said to him, 'To you I will give their glory and all this authority; for it has been given over to me, and I give it to anyone I please. If you, then, will worship me, it will all be yours.' Jesus answered him, 'It is written, 'Worship the Lord your God, and serve only him.''" (Luke 4:5-8). Jesus flatly refused all the wealth of the world. If worldly wealth is a sign of our heavenly Father's approval, Jesus would have been the wealthiest person of all time, for he is, without a doubt, the most approved of by our Father.

"...I exhort the elders among you to tend the flock of God that is in your charge, exercising the oversight, not under compulsion but willingly, as God would have you do it—not for sordid gain but eagerly. Do not lord it over those in your charge, but be examples to the flock."

1 Peter 5:1-3

Beware of pastors who use their pulpits to promote their social or political agendas. Their teaching is politically correct but morally obtuse. "…They speak visions of their own minds, not from the mouth of the Lord. They keep saying to those who despise the word of the Lord, 'It shall be well with you'; and to all who stubbornly follow their own stubborn hearts, they say, 'No calamity shall come upon you.'" (Jeremiah 23:16-17) Do not listen to these false prophets! Run from them before your heart is corrupted!

Beware of pastors who offer cures and favors from God and then coerce donations from the faithful. You've heard them. They offer healings or solutions to financial problems if only you will give more money to God; and they are happy to offer you an address to send it to or a basket to place it in. These pastors prey on the vulnerable and God's hopeful children. Anyone who thinks God exchanges his graces for money is very confused. God's grace cannot be bought. He gives his graces freely.

A clear example of God's condemnation of grace selling is the story of the above mentioned Simon the Magician. Simon witnessed Peter and John laying hands on those Philip baptized in Samaria who had not yet received the Holy Spirit. "Now when Simon saw that the Spirit was given through the laying on of the apostles' hands, he offered them money, saying, 'Give me also this power so that anyone on whom I lay my hands may receive the Holy Spirit.' But Peter said to him, 'May your silver perish with you, because you thought you could obtain God's gift with money! You have no part or share in this, for your heart is not right before God'" (Acts 8:18-21). Listen to Peter. If a pastor or televangelist says that your prayers will be answered or that you will receive favors from God if you make a donation, leave immediately, change the channel, and regard that false prophet as one whose "heart is not right before God."

Beware of pastors who corrupt Scripture to support sinful ideologies. God's Truth does not change over time! These corruptors allow scripture interpretation to be "modified" to soothe the conscience of the populace, which prefers the sin to God's Law. God's Law cannot be changed by legislation or popular opinion. God's Law is our freedom! These false prophets are teaching modern perversions instead of God's Word. They are anti-Christ!

The Good Pastor

A good pastor's life reflects the life of Jesus. Look at Jesus. He prayed often, lived simply, and owned only what he needed. He gratefully accepted what was offered and was humble enough to beg water from the Samaritan woman[3] at the well. Jesus helped all those who would accept his help. He provided food for the hungry crowds who came to hear him speak.[4] And when he was exhausted and grieving the death of John the Baptist, he still looked to the needs of those who came to hear his Word.[5] By his example of love, Jesus showed how he wanted his flock to be shepherded. A good pastor leads by example of loving obedience to the Gospel, speaks God's Word with courage, defies heresy, defends the Truth, and shares the Good News of God's love in word and deed. The good pastor strives to be like Jesus so that his flock will follow the example of Jesus.

A good pastor needs a faithful flock. It is an exercise in frustration for the good pastor when God's Word falls upon deaf ears and the faith of his flock changes like the wind. Paul the apostle had to deal with these problems. He spent time in Galatia teaching the Gospel of Christ. After he established the Christian church in Galatia, Paul traveled on but he kept in touch with the newly-founded church by letters. Soon Paul found it necessary to write the following to the Galatian converts: "I am astonished that you are so quickly deserting the one (God)[6] who called you in the grace of Christ and are turning to a different gospel—not that there is another gospel, but there are some who are confusing you and want to pervert the gospel of Christ" (Galatians 1:6-7). Some false teachers had told the Galatians that Baptism was not enough, and that all converts to Christianity had to pass through an intermediate stage of conversion to Judaism including rituals like circumcision. The Christian Galatians must have felt that Paul had not read them the "fine print" before they accepted Christ! They lost faith in the true gospel Paul taught them and became confused by trouble-making teachers who claimed their credentials were better than Paul's. Paul was forced to defend his authority to teach the gospel and made it clear that when he met with Peter, James, and John in Jerusalem, the decision was made by the Council of the Church that conversion to Judaism was not necessary to become a Christian.[7] From the First Commandment to the Tenth, a good pastor must constantly defend God's Word against worldly teachings that would deceive God's children. Teaching Scripture and correcting error is a never-ending task, but it is precisely in this work that the pastor and congregation grow in unity in the grace of Christ.

It's time to take a stand!

Will we, as Christians, take to heart "sound doctrine?"

Or will we reject Christ's truth, "suit our own desires" and "wander away to myths?"

The apostle Paul advised his disciple, Timothy, about the pitfalls of being a teacher of the Gospel. He told Timothy to "proclaim the message; be persistent whether the time is favorable or unfavorable; convince, rebuke, and encourage, with the utmost patience in teaching" (2 Timothy 4:2). Then Paul warned Timothy, "For the time is coming when people will not put up with sound doctrine, but having itching ears, they will accumulate for themselves teachers to suit their own desires, and will turn away from listening to the truth and wander away to myths" (2 Timothy 4:3-4). This bit of Scripture reads as if it was written today, not two thousand years ago. It's time to take a stand! Will we, as Christians, take to heart "sound doctrine?" Or will we reject Truth, "suit our own desires," and "wander away to myths?"

The Wannabees

Wannabees are people who half-heartedly aspire to a goal. Are you a "wannabe" follower of Jesus or a Christian? "As they were going along the road, someone said to him, 'I will follow you wherever you go.' And Jesus said to him, 'Foxes have holes, and birds of the air have nests; but the Son of Man has nowhere to lay his head.' To another he said, 'Follow me.' But he said, 'Lord, first let me go and bury my father.' But Jesus said to him, 'Let the dead bury their own dead; but as for you, go and proclaim the kingdom of God.' Another said, 'I will follow you, Lord; but let me first say farewell to those at my home.' Jesus said to him, 'No one who puts a hand to the plow and looks back is fit for the kingdom of God'" (Luke 9:57-62).

Are You Ready for the Challenge?

Does that sound harsh? Do you really think that God has much use for feel-good religion and wishy-washy commitment? Jesus challenges us to, "Be perfect, therefore, as your heavenly Father is perfect" (Matthew 5:48).

If we are willing to commit to the challenge, God helps us grow. To cultivate a perfect rose, the gardener must provide the right amount of sunshine and water, and prune the bush carefully, cutting off its less desirable attributes at the perfect time. So it is with us. Just as God purified the Israelites of their false gods in the desert before they could enter the Promised Land, he purifies and perfects us so we can enter into the kingdom Jesus promised us. And as he purifies and perfects us, he shares his joy and peace with us.

...And the Reward?

God's joy is not like the joy of the world. With each joy we experience in this world, there is anxiety attached. A new baby is a cause for great joy in a family, but there is also anxiety about its health, financial commitments, the adjustments the family will have to make, and the like. A wedding is a cause for joy, but it has its own set of anxieties. God's joy has no anxiety attached. It is a pure peace that we cannot experience without God. It is the way God meant things to be.

God made us so that we may know him and how much he loves us; so that we may choose to serve him by serving others; and so that we can be happy with him and share in his glory after our work in this life is finished. We get to know God and learn how he wants us to serve others by spending time with God in prayer. Christians can have God's amazing gifts of joy and peace in the midst of the turmoil of the world through prayer. It is worth the effort. (More about prayer later.) In the short time we reside here on earth, God educates, encourages, and comforts us as he ever guides us on toward holiness and the heavenly home Jesus went to prepare for us.

What Christians Do

There is so much confusion in Christianity. Name-only Christians, who refuse Jesus' message of self-sacrifice and forgiveness, have invented a self-serving, self-centered religion that is not Christian at all. Churches have become social clubs with the inherent competitive class structure. Christians "shop" for churches that suit their desires: social and business networking, shopping for a spouse, Sunday morning entertainment, and so on. God's Word is an afterthought, not the main event.

How did Christianity wander so far from its roots? This is the Christian Church: "Now the whole group of those who believed were of one heart and soul, and no one claimed private ownership of any possessions, but everything they owned was held in common. With great power the apostles gave their testimony to the resurrection of the Lord Jesus, and great grace was upon them all. There was not a needy person among them, for as many as owned lands or houses sold them and brought the proceeds of what was sold. They laid it at the apostles' feet, and it was distributed to each as any had need" (Acts 4:32-35). The first Christians, the ones who actually met Jesus and heard his voice, took care of each other, "and great grace was upon them all." They were eyewitnesses to the greatest act of charity ever performed, Christ's freely willed acceptance of crucifixion for the salvation of humankind. They took to heart the words of Jesus, "I give you a new commandment, that you love one another. Just as I have loved you, you also should love one another. By this everyone will know that you are my disciples, if you have love for one another" (John 13:34-35). The spirit of love manifested by the first Christians is the example for us to follow.

Socialism/Communism Is Not Christian

Christian charity is disturbing to people who do not understand that charity originates in God's generous love for us. Christianity is the opposite of the political systems known as Socialism and Communism. Let it be repeated: Christian charity opposes Socialism and Communism. Socialism/Communism involves the imposition of coercive civil law commanding the redistribution of the individual's earnings and property under the threat of punishment, ostensibly for the greater good. They are perversions that deny God's gifts of free will and freedom of conscience. Christians provide for others in the freedom of spirit that trust in God's love gives. The generosity of Christians flows from the love of Christ who dwells within each of them.

Take the First Step

Are you willing to follow the example of Jesus and be a transmitter of God's love? God wills to use your hands and feet to show his love to the world. In prayer, offer to help. Always look at the people God sends you with respect for their God-given human dignity. Never expect gratitude but know that God sees our hearts and no gift given by a loving heart is ever wasted. If you are in need, be willing to accept help as a gift from God and thank those who make the offer. True charity lies not only in the giving of gifts, but also in the grateful receiving of gifts. Giving away what we have earned and feel we deserve to enjoy requires us to leave our comfort zone, but Jesus did not promise us a life of ease on earth. It is precisely in this life that we have to work for the good of others. True Christian charity requires us to imitate the apostles, leave what is familiar and comfortable behind, and follow Jesus. Where are we going? Home to the place Jesus made for us, our true home in heaven. Why is it so difficult if God wants us be with him in heaven, and gives us the means to get there? Why does this go against our human nature? Those are very good questions with a very sad answer.

CHAPTER 2

Why is it so Difficult?

· ·

Since childhood I have been told that Jesus died to save me. I knew the gruesome Crucifixion story and the story of the Resurrection, but just exactly what did that have to do with me? Why did I have to be redeemed? I was just a little kid. What had I done that was so evil that Jesus had to die for me? I was reminded of my sins and how much they hurt God. I was sure I didn't want to hurt God! Jesus had died to redeem me! All I knew about redemption was that Mom bought stuff with Green Stamps[8] at the Redemption Center. But I was certain I had heard my teachers correctly. I had been redeemed.

After I had grown in understanding through the Holy Spirit, I realized that the answer to my question was in the first book of the Bible, Genesis. God created an entire universe, complete with stars, sun, moon, land and water, plants and animals, and gave charge of it to two special creatures that he made in his own "likeness,"[9] Adam and Eve. Adam and Eve dwelt securely in Eden, the garden God made for them. "God saw everything that he had made, and indeed, it was very good…" (Genesis 1:31). Adam and Eve walked with God, and they understood their dependence upon him.

God created Adam and Eve to be his children, not his slaves, so he gave them free wills. God is love, the source of all love, and the end of all love. There is no love without him. He wanted them to freely choose to love him, and to that end, he gave them a test. He forbade them to eat the fruit of the Tree of Knowledge of Good and Evil.[10] It was not a deprivation for everything else in Eden was theirs. God did not make Adam and Eve like animals that cannot reason, but with the free will to love God and live as his friends—or not.

But Adam and Eve were sought out by God's old enemy, Satan. They accepted a proposal from Satan and ate the forbidden fruit. Clearly, this was an act of treason! Adam and Eve rejected God's love and generosity in favor of Satan's empty promises, the first time for humankind but not the last. When God came to visit them in the garden, he asked Adam and Eve what they had done. Adam blamed Eve, and implicitly God for creating her, and Eve blamed Satan.[11] By their disobedience, Adam and Eve threw all of creation into disorder, including themselves, for they were now pointing fingers at each other, no longer living in peaceful union.[12]

In his justice, God told Adam and Eve the consequences of their betrayal and they regretted their sin. Because of their heartfelt sorrow and shame, humankind did not suffer the same fate as the disobedient Lucifer, a.k.a. Satan, and his bad angels who lost heaven for all eternity.[13] But Adam and Eve chose Satan and so, just like the bad angels who chose to follow Satan, Adam, Eve and their children belonged to him. Satan figured he had outsmarted God! Because of their rejection of God's goodness, Adam and Eve suffered the loss of Eden, the preternatural graces,[14] and the unique one-on-one connection with God they had enjoyed. They now had to live in an unnatural world. They suffered loss of the knowledge God had given them with no effort on their part, a loss of control over their own passions, and they suffered illness and death. As sons and daughters of Adam and Eve, we inherit the consequences of their disobedience. Because of disobedience, all human nature is in chaos and beset with evil, deceit, sin, and death, the legacy of Satan. Since God gave Adam and Eve authority over all creation, it, too, was thrown into chaos and suffers the effects of the first sin. Because we inherit their human condition, we also sin.

Next time you are tempted to disobedience, remember the awful consequences of Adam and Eve's disobedience. One moment of disobedience could have tragic, unimaginable consequences. Adam and Eve never imagined that a bite of the forbidden fruit would cost so much in human pain and suffering, and result in the Son of God becoming man to suffer the wrath of Satan, crucifixion, and death to redeem us.

Free Will 101

Obedience is not a dirty word! We choose to obey human laws for our own welfare and for the public safety. We teach our children to obey rules for their well-being. Because of the compassion God had for Israel, he gave his Law to Moses to help them put order into their lives and teach them the way God meant for them to live—in security and happiness. But Israel often failed to obey Mosaic Law. There was confusion because the kings of Israel and Judah led their people with different degrees of devotion to God. Whether the kings worshipped God or pagan idols sometimes depended on which god their wives or mothers worshipped. God wanted his children to know him as the one true God and to live his Law so they could have his peace, but self-serving, false prophets led Israel and Judah into sin.

Nevertheless, God did not abandon his people. He sent them prophets, like Jeremiah, who tried to turn his people away from the worship of false gods. Jeremiah was a young man when God sent him to Judah to accuse the people of rejecting God's graces. Time and again, God told Jeremiah to prophesy to his people that their actions were leading them to terrible consequences. Jeremiah was the early warning system of his time. For example: "The word that came to Jeremiah from the Lord: 'Stand in the gate of the Lord's house, and proclaim there this word, and say, Hear the word of the Lord, all you people of Judah, you that enter these gates to worship the Lord. Thus says the Lord of hosts, the God of Israel: Amend your ways and doings, and let me dwell with you in this place. Do not trust in these deceptive words: 'This is the temple of the Lord, the temple of the Lord, the temple of the Lord.' For if you truly amend your ways and your doings, if you truly act justly one with another, if you do not oppress the alien, the orphan, and the widow, or shed innocent blood in this place, and if you do not go after other gods to your own hurt, then I will dwell with you in this place, in the land that I gave of old to your ancestors forever and ever. Here you are, trusting in deceptive words to no avail. Will you steal, murder, commit adultery, swear falsely, make offerings to Baal, and go after other gods that you have not known, and then come and stand before me in this house, which is called by my name, and say, 'We are safe!'—only to go on doing all these abominations? Has this house, which is called by my name, become a den of robbers in your sight? You know, I too am watching, says the Lord'" (Jeremiah 7:1-11). Through Jeremiah, God warned his people against the arrogant hypocrisy of believing that they were protected against the consequences of their sinful actions because they proclaimed themselves as chosen by the one true God and worshipped in his temple.

But look at the promise! If only Israel would obey God's commandments, they would enjoy God's presence and protection forever and ever. However, the people did not heed God's words, rejected him, and Jerusalem was destroyed.

Fast-forward about six centuries: "Then someone came to him and said, 'Teacher, what good deed must I do to have eternal life?' And he said to him, 'Why do you ask me about what is good? There is only one who is good. If you wish to enter into life, keep the commandments.' He said to him, 'Which ones?' And Jesus said, 'You shall not murder; You shall not commit adultery; You shall not steal; You shall not bear false witness; Honor your father and mother; also, You shall love your neighbor as yourself.' The young man said to him, 'I have kept all these; what do I still lack?'

Jesus said to him, 'If you wish to be perfect, go, sell your possessions, and give the money to the poor, and you will have treasure in heaven; then come, follow me.' When the young man heard this word, he went away grieving, for he had many possessions" (Matthew19:16-22). This young man had kept the commandments but by his question, "What do I still lack?" there is a sense that he wants to be closer to God. He wants more, so Jesus offers him the path to perfection and the young man goes away sad because he cannot part with his possessions. It is easy to second-guess this young man's reaction but harder to know how we would react if asked the same question. We do not know if the young man re-thought his initial reaction and later became a disciple. We do know that he rejected this call to "Come, follow me."

Choices

What do these stories have in common? There were choices to be made. Adam and Eve lived in paradise, but they chose apples. Jeremiah told Israel that God offered them his presence and protection forever if they would only stop their sinful actions and obey the commandments. They chose to reject God's offer, lost his protection, and Jerusalem was destroyed. The young man was offered perfection by Jesus and he went away grieving because he chose not to make the commitment required. In the exercise of their free wills, all of these people took their focus off eternal life and settled for short-term false promises.

But with our busy lives and so many responsibilities, how do we keep our focus on God? Isn't it in our basic nature to settle for what is easy, for what we can see? How do we discipline our free will? Why do we make foolish choices that cause us problems on earth and could cost us eternal happiness? Jesus came to show us a new way of life, and to bring a new grace into the world. He came to give us the answer. He came to show us the immensity of God's love for us. So who is this Jesus we are expected to follow?

CHAPTER 3

Who is Jesus?

· ·

W ho is Jesus? How do we know he is the Messiah? Why do we believe that he is God, the co-eternal son of our Father? Did God really become man?

Jesus' story is much longer than thirty-three years. His story is eternal—always has been and always will be. But eternal is a bit hard for us to grasp, so we will concern ourselves with the manageable length of time detailed in the Bible.

The story of Noah is now the stuff of children's bedtime stories, but its importance must not be diminished.

Firstly, it exemplifies God's great mercy to those who remain steadfastly faithful.

Secondly, it is a clear example of God's justice, demonstrates that the choices we make have consequences, and that God's forgiveness must not be taken for granted.

Thirdly, the ark is symbolic of the Christian Church as a place of refuge amid the great evils in this world.

Fourthly, the flood waters represent the waters of Baptism, which cleanse our souls from all sin as the earth was cleansed from evil.

"In the beginning" are the first words of the Book of Genesis and the Gospel of John[15] so let's begin:

"In the beginning"

"In the beginning" of Genesis, Adam and Eve chose Satan's false promises and humankind suffered the sad consequences. But Satan did not get away with his evil deed. God told Satan: "I will put enmity between you and the woman, and between your offspring and hers; he will strike at your head, and you will strike at his heel" (Genesis 3:15). With these words, God our Father foretold our redemption through Jesus, the "offspring" of Mary, "the woman"—a curse to Satan, and hope for humankind. "Everyone who commits sin is a child of the devil; for the devil has been sinning from the beginning. The Son of God was revealed for this purpose, to destroy the works of the devil" (1 John 3:8). Unrepentant sinners have "itching ears," "turn away from listening to the truth and wander away to myths." They are the "children of the devil."[16] Children of God regret sin, enjoy God's forgiveness, and the everlasting happiness Jesus won for us. However, like Adam and Eve, humankind often does not cooperate with God's plan for everlasting happiness.

Lost by Disobedience...
By Obedience Won

After a time, humankind willfully drifted so far away from God that they were no longer recognizable as the people he created. They were the true living dead, walking around and breathing, but with souls so dead that they were rotting and oozing all kinds of evil. God was horrified at how inhuman humankind had become. Noah's generation spent their energy rejecting God's grace. God could not allow the evil to continue. "But Noah found favor in the sight of the Lord" (Genesis 6:8). So God gave Noah detailed ark-building instructions. Unlike Adam and Eve,

Noah *obeyed* God's Will and thereby preserved humankind and the animals of the earth.[17] After the ark was boarded, the flood came. People who were already dead in their sin were destroyed. In their wickedness, they destroyed themselves. Noah's progeny repopulated the earth and about ten generations later, Abram/Abraham was born.

"Now the Lord said to Abram, 'Go from your country and your kindred and your father's house to the land that I will show you. I will make of you a great nation, and I will bless you, and make your name great, so that you will be a blessing. I will bless those who bless you, and the one who curses you I will curse; and in you all the families of the earth shall be blessed" (Genesis 12:1-3). God gave Abram a new name—Abraham. Abraham left his home and followed God's Will. He became "a great nation."[18] And the blessing, that God promised "all the families of the earth" through Abraham, was fulfilled in Jesus Christ, a son of Abraham, who commissioned the apostles to spread the Gospel to the ends of the earth.

In Abraham's day, pagans practiced ritual human sacrifice. First-born children were sacrificed to pagan gods in Canaan, the land in which Abraham lived.[19] God asked Abraham to sacrifice his son, Isaac. Abraham proved his trust in God by *obediently* preparing his beloved son, the only child of his wife, Sarah, to be sacrificed as God requested. At the last moment, God sent an angel to intervene and provide a ram to be sacrificed in Isaac's place.[20] The effect was a kind of show and tell. By forbidding Abraham to sacrifice his son, God essentially forbade human sacrifice.

Some centuries later, Jewish priests convened the Sanhedrin to discuss the fate of God's Son, Jesus. They feared that he would cause them problems with their Roman conquerors. The high priest, Caiaphas, told the Sanhedrin: "You do not understand that it is better for you to have one man die for the people than to have the whole nation destroyed." "So from that day on they planned to put him to death" (John 11:50, 53). Unlike their ancestor Abraham, the chief priests trusted in their own power instead of God's for the salvation of Israel. They plotted a heinous act of treason against God when they offered Jesus as a human sacrifice to protect themselves from the Romans, but by God's Will, Jesus' sacrifice became eternal salvation for all humankind.

After Abraham's death, Isaac left his home because of famine and decided to take his family to Egypt. But while he was in the land of the Philistines, "The Lord appeared to Isaac and said, 'Do not go down to Egypt; settle in the land that I shall show you. Reside in this land as an alien, and I will be with you, and will bless you; for to you and to your descendants I will give all these lands, and I will fulfill the oath that I swore to your father Abraham'" (Genesis 26:2-3). Isaac *obeyed* God's Will and the Covenant God made to Abraham continued in Isaac.

God told Isaac's son, Jacob, to go to Bethel and Jacob *obeyed* God's Will. At Bethel, God repeated his Covenant to Jacob and renamed him Israel.[21] Jacob/Israel had twelve sons and from these sons descended the twelve tribes, the Israelite people.

Then in a strange turn of events, the Israelite people ended up settling in Egypt. The thumbnail version goes like this: Israel's sons were jealous of their brother Joseph and sold him to Midianite traders, who took him to Egypt and sold him to one of Pharaoh's officials. Because God gave Joseph the gift of interpreting dreams, he came to the attention of Pharaoh who made him overseer of the land of Egypt. In his position of authority, Joseph was able to bring his entire family to Egypt where he helped them survive seven years of famine, and they were comfortable in Egypt for hundreds of years.[22] Until another Pharaoh, fearing the growing strength of the Israelite people, forgot Egypt's promise to Joseph,[23] ordered the murder of all male Israelite newborns, and forced the Israelites into slavery. Then Moses, an Israelite baby saved from the death sentence and raised in the house of Pharaoh, *obeyed* God who spoke to him from a burning bush. Through Moses, God performed ten miracles of plagues, each one worse than the last, to convince Pharaoh to release the Israelites. By his *obedience* to God's Will, Moses rescued his people so that they could be free to know and worship the one true God.

God chose Moses for the task of leading his people. Moses should have been murdered like the all the other Israelite male babies. Instead, he was rescued by Pharaoh's daughter and raised in Pharaoh's household as her son. He received education and skills that uniquely qualified him to plead for the freedom of the Israelites. But Moses had a free will. What if he had chosen not to cooperate with God's Will? Would there even be an Israelite people now? Where would salvation history be? Would we still be waiting for the Messiah?

God willed the Israelites to be his chosen people. Through Moses, God freed them, gave them the Ten Commandments, a tribal governmental structure, miraculous food (manna), water from a rock, and guided them to the Promised Land. But, the Israelite people were not always cooperative. God did not intend that the Israelites wander in the desert for forty years, but when the people refused to trust God, they suffered the consequence of their actions. Before they crossed over into Canaan, God instructed Moses to send spies into the Promised Land. For forty days they scouted, and all of the spies, except Joshua and Caleb, brought back scary stories of monster-sized, well-armed, well-entrenched natives. "And all the Israelites complained against Moses and Aaron; the whole congregation said to them, 'Would that we had died in the land of Egypt! Or would that we had died in this wilderness! Why is the Lord bringing us into this land to fall by the sword? Our wives and our little ones will become booty; would it not be better for us to go back to Egypt?' So they said to one another, 'Let us choose a captain and go back to Egypt.'" (Numbers 14:2-4). The ever-patient Moses and Aaron prayed to God to forgive his people. "Then the Lord said, 'I do forgive, just as you have asked; nevertheless—as I live, and as all the earth shall be filled with the glory of the Lord—none of the people who have seen my glory and the signs that I did in Egypt and in the wilderness, and yet have tested me these ten times and have not obeyed my voice, shall see the land that I swore to give to their ancestors; none of those who despised me shall see it.'" (Numbers 14:20-23). "But your little ones, who you said would become booty, I will bring in, and they shall know the land that you have despised. But as for you, your dead bodies shall fall in this wilderness. And your children shall be shepherds in the wilderness for forty years, and shall suffer for your faithlessness, until the last of your dead bodies lies in the wilderness. According to the number of days in which you spied out the land, forty days, for every day a year, you shall bear your iniquity, forty years, and you shall know my displeasure" (Numbers 14:31-34).

Entry into the Promised Land was denied to the rebels, not out of vengeance, but because they threatened the peace and wellbeing of the Israelite people. When Moses told the Israelite rebels what God said, they decided to go into Canaan anyway. Read Numbers 14:39-45 for the rest of that story. The two spies who spoke honestly about Canaan? After the forty years, Joshua led the Israelites into Canaan and, with the help of God, conquered the land. Caleb was given Hebron for his faithfulness. See the Book of Joshua for the full story.

In the fullness of time, the grace of God, lost by Adam's disobedience, was restored to us by Christ's obedience.

In spite of their disobedience, God never abandoned the Israelites. They knew God was always with them no matter where they went. God instructed them to build the Ark of the Covenant to house the tablets of the Ten Commandments, thereby teaching them to honor the Word of God. God had them build a portable tent of worship where he met face to face with Moses.[24] He designated Moses' brother, Aaron, as the first High Priest

---

and appointed Aaron's sons as priests. Then, working within the scope of their experiences, God instructed his people through Moses in various rites of worship.[25] Worship commonly included animal sacrifices and, although uncomfortable to our sensibilities, the ancient Israelites understood these offerings as religious practices. One example: God instructed his priests to offer a ritual animal sacrifice to atone for sin so that the Israelites would have a visible sign to assure them that their sins were forgiven. God wanted the Israelites to understand his limitless mercy toward those who love him. God said to Moses, "And you shall bring to the priest, as your guilt offering to the Lord, a ram without blemish from the flock, or its equivalent, for a guilt offering. The priest shall make atonement on your behalf before the Lord, and you shall be forgiven for any of the things that one may do and incur guilt thereby" (Leviticus 6:6-7).

Ancient Israel's worship is not without meaning for Christians. Jesus Christ is the guilt offering, once and for all. He is the Lamb of God, who was sacrificed so that we who believe in him "shall be forgiven for any of the things that one may do and incur guilt thereby." John the Baptist testifies to this: "The next day he saw Jesus coming toward him and declared, 'Here is the Lamb of God who takes away the sin of the world!'" (John 1:29).

Broken, sinful humankind could not restore itself to grace. Like a disease that damages the body and limits movement, the movements of grace in the human soul were damaged by sin. Christ came to heal damaged souls. God's plan for humankind's return to grace took millennia to accomplish through his obedient servants who prepared the way for Christ.

The God-Man Foretold

"In the beginning" of John's Gospel, the hope for regaining paradise is fulfilled in the person of Jesus Christ. John tells us exactly who Jesus is: "In the beginning was the Word, and the Word was with God, and the Word was God" (John 1:1). "And the Word became flesh and lived among us, and we have seen his glory, the glory as of a father's only son, full of grace and truth" (John 1:14). "He came to what was his own, and his own people did not accept him. But to all who received him, who believed in his name, he gave power to become children of God, who were born, not of blood or of the will of the flesh or of the will of man, but of God" (John 1:11-13)

"The Word became flesh..." God had already revealed some mysteries about himself in the Messianic prophesies recorded in Hebrew Scripture, but much remained hidden including the mystery of eternal life. For example, the Pharisees believed in life after death, but the Sadducees did not, and nobody knew for sure. God chose the time and place to reveal to humankind the mysteries of his eternal plan. The time was so important that calendars stopped and a new era began. The place, Bethlehem, was revealed in Hebrew Scripture so that all humankind would recognize the expected Messiah when he came.

Jesus is the Promised One, the Word made flesh, the fulfillment of Hebrew prophecy, the Messiah. Here are just a few examples of evidence the Gospels give concerning Jesus as the Messiah:

When Joseph realized that his betrothed Mary was pregnant, he felt betrayed and decided to divorce her quietly. "But just when he had resolved to do this, an angel of the Lord appeared to him in a dream and said, 'Joseph, son of David, do not be afraid to take Mary as your wife, for the child conceived in her is from the Holy Spirit. She will bear a son, and you are to name him Jesus, for he will save his people from their sins.' All this took place to fulfill what had been spoken by the Lord through the prophet: 'Look, the virgin shall conceive and bear a son, and they shall name him Emmanuel,' which means, 'God is with us'" (Matthew 1:20-23).

When Herod the Great asked the chief priests where the Messiah was to be born, "They told him, 'In Bethlehem of Judea; for so it has been written by the prophet: 'And you, Bethlehem, in the land of Judah, are by no means least among the rulers of Judah; for from you shall come a ruler who is to shepherd my people Israel.''" (Matthew 2:5-6).

"Jesus told the crowds all these things in parables; without a parable he told them nothing. This was to fulfill what had been spoken through the prophet: 'I will open my mouth to speak in parables; I will proclaim what has been hidden from the foundation of the world'" (Matthew 13:34-35).

"When they had come near Jerusalem and had reached Bethphage, at the Mount of Olives, Jesus sent two disciples, saying to them, 'Go into the village ahead of you, and immediately you will find a donkey tied, and a colt with her; untie them and bring them to me. If anyone says anything to you, just say this, 'The Lord needs them.' And he will send them immediately.' This took place to fulfill what had been spoken through the prophet, saying, 'Tell the daughter of Zion, Look, your king is coming to you, humble and mounted on a donkey, and on a colt, the foal of a donkey'" (Matthew 21:1-5). Jesus entered Jerusalem riding on a donkey on Palm Sunday.

Jesus declared himself to be the fulfillment of Messianic prophecy, "When he came to Nazareth, where he had been brought up, he went to the synagogue on the sabbath day, as was his custom. He stood up to read, and the scroll of the prophet Isaiah was given to him. He unrolled the scroll and found the place where it was written: 'The Spirit of the Lord is upon me, because he has anointed me to bring good news to the poor. He has sent me to proclaim release to the captives and recovery of sight to the blind, to let the oppressed go free, to proclaim the year of the Lord's favor.' And he rolled up the scroll, gave it back to the attendant, and sat down. The eyes of all in the synagogue were fixed on him. Then he began to say to them, 'Today this scripture has been fulfilled in your hearing'" (Luke 4:16-21).

For the Jews, the testimony of two witnesses was adequate to determine the truth in a matter. The Hebrew Bible is replete with testimonies to the

Messiah and foretells Jesus' identity, birth, life, death, and purpose. Isaiah 53 and Psalm 22 are just two examples. During his life on earth, Jesus' disciples and many eyewitnesses testified that he is the Christ, and then after his Resurrection, the fulfillment of the Old Testament prophecies were made clear in the Gospels, epistles, and pastoral letters. Christians must read the Old Testament to understand how God prepared humankind for the coming of the Christ.

Jesus Is Truly God...

The Gospels state that Jesus is the Messiah, the Son of God, and the Savior whose coming was foretold:

Luke's Gospel tells the story of Mary, a young virgin engaged to be married, and the miraculous turn her life took when God's messenger, the Archangel Gabriel, appeared to her and told her, "And now, you will conceive in your womb and bear a son, and you will name him Jesus. He will be great, and will be called the Son of the Most High..." (Luke 1:31-32).

When Jesus was only three months in Mary's womb, Zechariah, the father of John the Baptist prophesied that God had "...raised up a mighty savior for us in the house of his servant David, as he spoke through the mouth of his holy prophets from of old" (Luke 1:69-70). Then, he said of his newborn son, John: "And you, child, will be called the prophet of the Most High; for you will go before the Lord to prepare his ways" (Luke 1:76). John the Baptist recognized and bore witness to Jesus as Jesus began his work.

When Jesus was born, an angel appeared to shepherds tending their flocks and said, "...Do not be afraid; for see–I am bringing you good news of great joy for all the people: to you is born this day in the city of David a Savior, who is the Messiah, the Lord'" (Luke 2:10-11).

In the temple at Jerusalem, Simeon, the righteous and devout man,[26] and Anna, a prophet,[27] recognized the infant Jesus was the Messiah. Twelve years later, Jesus, himself, gave testimony to his identity as the Son of God, the Messiah when Mary and Joseph found Jesus in the temple. Mary asked Jesus why he had disappeared. "He said to them, 'Why were you searching for me? Did you not know that I must be in my Father's house?'" (Luke 2:49).

When Jesus taught at the temple treasury, indignant scribes and Pharisees demanded to know exactly who Jesus claimed to be! An angry debate ensued. "Jesus answered, 'If I glorify myself, my glory is nothing. It is my Father who glorifies me, he of whom you say, 'He is our God,' though you do not know him. But I know him; if I would say that I do not know him, I would be a liar like you. But I do know him and I keep his word. Your ancestor Abraham rejoiced that he would see my day; he saw it and was glad.' Then the Jews said to him, 'You are not yet fifty years old, and you have seen Abraham?' Jesus said to them, 'Very truly, I tell you, before Abraham was, I am'" (John 8:54-58). The Jewish leaders understood exactly what Jesus meant and became very angry. When Jesus stated that he existed before Abraham and referred to himself by the name of God, I AM,[28] he was saying that he is the Messiah and co-eternal with the Father. But, in the simplicity of his lifestyle, Jesus did not fit their idea of the Son of God. "So they picked up stones to throw at him, but Jesus hid himself and went out of the Temple" (John 8:59). Jewish law prescribed: "One who blasphemes the name of the Lord shall be put to death; the whole congregation shall stone the blasphemer..." (Leviticus 24:16). By picking up the stones, the Jewish leaders were accusing Jesus of blasphemy and recognizing that Jesus claimed to be the Son of God. But they were the blasphemers. They refused to accept Jesus as their Messiah. Jesus was outraged at the Jewish leaders who knew Scripture but perverted it to suit their own desires. Jesus warned the Jewish leaders that they were children of the devil, the father of lies, and the Jewish leaders accused Jesus of having a demon! Read John 8 for the entire lively exchange.

Again, after Jesus was arrested, he was brought before the Jewish chief priests and elders and questioned. "…Again the high priest asked him, 'Are you the Messiah, the Son of the Blessed One?' Jesus said, 'I am; and 'you will see the Son of Man seated at the right hand of the Power,' and 'coming with the clouds of heaven'" (Mark 14:61-62).

Considering the healings and miracles Jesus performed, the clarity of his teaching, the testimony of many eyewitnesses to his resurrection from the dead, and ascension into heaven, and the testimony of Stephen, the first Christian martyr, who told his murderers, "'Look,' he said, 'I see the heavens opened and the Son of Man standing at the right hand of God!'" (Acts 7:56). Clearly, there is ample testimony to the divinity of Jesus.

…and Jesus Is Truly Man

Jesus was born of a woman like all men. He walked, talked, worked, and dealt with relatives like any other man. He was circumcised on the eighth day and was presented to our Father in the temple, like other first-born Jewish male children. He grew hungry and tired, got irritated with his friends, and knew happiness and anxiety, and anger at God's enemies. He grieved over the deaths of John the Baptist and his friend Lazarus. Jesus was born, lived and died.

Yet some people denied the humanity of Jesus. This question of faith was resolved by a consensus of legitimate successors of Jesus' apostles in the power of the Holy Spirit. There was no Bible as we know it when the Church began. The apostles and disciples used letters, newly-written gospels and the guidance of the Holy Spirit to spread the faith and maintain its integrity. They were vigilant to protect the faith Jesus taught them from heretics, but there were honest disagreements. Fortunately, the apostles left a blueprint for resolving questions of faith. When some formerly Jewish Christians thought that Gentiles should be required to convert to Judaism before conversion to Christianity, there was genuine disagreement between

Gentile and Jewish Christians. In Jerusalem, "The apostles and elders met together to consider this matter" (Acts 15:6). Read Acts 15:1-29 for a look into the spirit of the discussions and decisions made by those who were closest to Christ. These are the decisions Paul wrote about to the Galatians when he told them that conversion to Judaism was an unnecessary step.

For three centuries, the Church suffered persecutions and many Christians were martyred under pagan emperors for heresy because Christians would not offer sacrifices to the pagan gods. Finally, Emperor Constantine issued his Edict of Milan in 313 that legalized Christianity. Christians could now meet in peace to talk about matters of faith. A meeting of the bishops was organized to address issues regarding uniformity of Church doctrine. The Council of Nicaea, the first Ecumenical Council of the universal Christian Church was called in 325 A.D. In this blessed new era of peace, three hundred and eighteen bishops met together to unify and defend the faith handed down from Jesus through the apostles and their successors, and to combat heretical teachings, particularly the heresy of Arius (Aryanism) which had caused confusion, division, and factions within the Church. Arius claimed that God the Father alone is eternal and that Jesus is not God and not co-eternal, but a lesser being. The three hundred and eighteen bishops debated the ideas of Arius, with Arius himself presenting his argument to the Council. The Council's decision is the following affirmation of the humanity and divinity of Jesus:

"We believe in one God the Father Almighty, Maker of all things visible and invisible; and in one Lord Jesus Christ, the only begotten of the Father, that is, of the substance of the Father, God of God, light of light, true God of true God, begotten not made, of the same substance with the Father, through whom all things were made both in heaven and on earth; who for us men and our salvation descended, was incarnate, and was made man, suffered and rose again on the third day, ascended into heaven and cometh to judge the living and the dead. And in the Holy Ghost. Those who say: There was a time when He was not, and He was not before He was begotten; and that He was made out of nothing; or who maintain that He is of another hypostasis or another substance [than the Father], or that the Son of God is created, or mutable, or subject to change, [them] the Catholic Church anathematizes." (Leclercq)

The teachings of Arius were judged heretical by the bishops of the Church. Arius and his followers who continued to teach heresy were anathematized, that is, excommunicated. The conclusion of the Council of Nicaea, that Jesus is God and is of the same essence (hypostasis) and nature as God the Father Almighty and co-eternal with him, remains a basic and unchangeable tenet of Christianity. The above statement of faith, originally formulated to correct Arian heresy, was expanded upon in later Councils to include tenets of faith regarding the Holy Spirit and the Trinitarian nature of God, the universality of the Church, and more. Belief in the tenets of the Nicene Creed developed by the Church Fathers to protect Christ's teachings is the basic requirement for all who call themselves Christian. Any persons or groups who deny these tenets and call themselves Christian are frauds.

CHAPTER 4

Jesus Proclaims the Kingdom of God

"Jesus went throughout Galilee, teaching in their synagogues and proclaiming the good news of the kingdom and curing every disease and every sickness among the people. So his fame spread throughout all Syria, and they brought to him all the sick, those who were afflicted with various diseases and pains, demoniacs, epileptics, and paralytics, and he cured them. And great crowds followed him from Galilee, the Decapolis, Jerusalem, Judea, and from beyond the Jordan" (Matthew 4:23-25).

Jesus came to earth as our Redeemer to pay the debt for our sin, and to make known to us our heavenly inheritance. He wants to share his kingdom with us now. Yes, NOW! "We have this hope, a sure and steadfast anchor of the soul, a hope that enters the inner shrine behind the curtain, where Jesus, a forerunner on our behalf, has entered, having become a high priest forever according to the order of Melchizedek" (Hebrews 6:19-20). Paul tells us that our hope "enters the inner shrine behind the curtain," which, in the Temple, was the place for the Holy of Holies, the place where God was present. We are invited to enter that sacred place where love takes us into the presence of God. We can peek behind the curtain of "the inner shrine" while we live on this earth through prayer and contemplation, that is speaking and listening to our loving God.

People followed Jesus hoping to be healed of their ailments "and he cured them." Hope brought them to Christ, and their faith grew from the power of having their hopes realized.

We, too, are invited to follow Jesus in hope into the "inner shrine" to be healed of our sins and grow in faith until Christ fully realizes our hopes in the Kingdom of God.

Are you thinking, "Who am I to enter the 'inner shrine'?" Revelation 1:4-6 tells us, "…Grace to you and peace … from Jesus Christ, the faithful witness, the firstborn of the dead, and the ruler of the kings of the earth. To him who loves us and freed us from our sins by his blood, and made us to be a kingdom, priests serving his God and Father, to him be glory and dominion forever and ever. Amen." Jesus "made us to be a kingdom, priests serving his God and Father." We each own an individual priesthood so that our prayers and sacrifices may serve God as Jesus' did. We have a call and a duty to follow Jesus into the "inner shrine behind the curtains"!

Where Do We Start?

Jesus tells us:

Repent and have faith: "Now after John was arrested, Jesus came to Galilee, proclaiming the good news of God, and saying, 'The time is fulfilled, and the kingdom of God has come near; repent, and believe in the good news'" (Mark:1:14-15).

Love God and love your neighbor: As Jesus was speaking to the scribes, "One of the scribes came near and heard them disputing with one another, and seeing that he answered them well, he asked him, 'Which commandment is the first of all?' Jesus answered, 'The first is, 'Hear, O Israel: the

Lord our God, the Lord is one; you shall love the Lord your God with all your heart, and with all your soul, and with all your mind, and with all your strength.' The second is this, 'You shall love your neighbor as yourself.' There is no greater commandment than these.' Then the scribe said to him, 'You are right, Teacher; you have truly said that 'he is one, and besides him there is no other'; and 'to love him with all the heart, and with all the understanding, and with all the strength,' and 'to love one's neighbor as oneself,'–this is much more important than all whole burnt offerings and sacrifices.' When Jesus saw that he answered wisely, he said to him, 'You are not far from the kingdom of God'..." (Mark 12:28-34). These verses start us on our journey into the kingdom "not of this world." We prepare for God's kingdom through repentance and conversion of heart. Repentance means that we must regret our words, thoughts, and actions that offend God's love, and make a serious effort not to be a repeat offender. We must also make amends for our offenses. Conversion of heart means that we must desire God's law of love more than anything in this world. We must love God with all of the passion our hearts can muster, and strive to know him with every ounce of enthusiasm in our beings. In addition, we must love others, and treat them as well as we love and treat ourselves. And that includes the people we do not like!

Trust in God's grace: God gives us abundant grace and strength to live our Christian vocations, so we can accomplish our desires and efforts to love him and seek his wisdom. All we have to do is ask! "If you then, who are evil, know how to give good gifts to your children, how much more will the heavenly Father give the Holy Spirit to those who ask him?" (Luke 11:13).

Keep God's Commandments: "Judas (not Iscariot) said to him, 'Lord, how is it that you will reveal yourself to us, and not to the world?' Jesus answered him, 'Those who love me will keep my word, and my Father will love them, and we will come to them and make our home with them" (John

14:22-23). Not only that! Jesus also promised, "If you love me, you will keep my commandments. And I will ask the Father, and he will give you another Advocate, to be with you forever. This is the Spirit of truth, whom the world cannot receive, because it neither sees him nor knows him. You know him, because he abides with you, and he will be in you" (John 14:15-17). The Father, the Son, and the Holy Spirit, the Holy Trinity, abiding with us, making his home with us forever! This is God's promise and our hope, "a hope that enters the inner shrine behind the curtain" to draw us closer to God, starting from where we are in our lives right now!

These understandings are both the beginning and the fullness of our adventure into the Kingdom of God. Does God really want to be so near to us? Those are the words of Jesus in the Gospels, which are Truth! Anyone who does not accept the Gospels as Truth has no foundation for understanding this Guide.

Jesus as Brother, Friend

Just like any worthwhile relationship, our friendship with Jesus requires some effort. It pleases our living, loving, interactive Jesus when we remember him during the day as we work, play, make decisions, care for our families, talk to friends, and so on. He wants to share our lives with us. He wants to communicate with us. Jesus offers us the ultimate social network, communicating with the Holy Trinity, and it doesn't even require an app! He waits for us to love and trust him so that we can live the way he meant for us to live, in peace and security. He wants us to grow closer to him and the perfect joy of eternal life.

God communicates with us on many levels. Once we accept his invitation to "enter the inner shrine behind the curtain," we become open to the inspirations of the Holy Spirit. We begin to recognize God at work in our lives. Don't be surprised at feelings of sorrow for offending God as we come to know how very much he loves us. But then, God comforts us and gives us peace which follows from the knowledge of, or more clearly, the personal certainty of his mercy and forgiveness. His loving kindness and the joy it gives draws us to love him even more. As we grow nearer to God, spiritual changes occur and wisdom increases. Virtues and understanding increase, sometimes suddenly, like a teenage boy's growth spurt, and sometimes by little baby steps. True happiness, joy, and peace can only come from knowledge of God. That is a fact. There will be obstacles. The devil, the flesh, and the world challenge our spiritual progress, but overcoming these obstacles increases our grace and strength to fight the battles ahead on our path to heaven.

World at War

The world is at war. Millions of battles are fought every day. The prize is not land or power or money; it is the destiny of each human soul. The combatants are loving souls, who cooperate with God's grace, versus complacent and dead souls, who reject grace and cooperate with Satan. Scripture reveals that the victory belongs to those who follow Christ, but souls who choose darkness and lies are blind to Scripture's Truth. "For the wrath of God is revealed from heaven against all ungodliness and wickedness of those who by their wickedness suppress the truth. For what can be known about God is plain to them, because God has shown it to them. Ever since the creation of the world his eternal power and divine nature, invisible though they are, have been understood and seen through the things he has made. So they are without excuse; for though they knew God, they did not honor him as God or give thanks to him, but they became futile in their thinking, and their senseless minds were darkened. Claiming to be wise, they became fools; and they exchanged the glory of the immortal God for images resembling a mortal human being or birds or four-footed animals or reptiles. Therefore God gave them up in the lusts of their hearts to impurity, to the degrading of their bodies among themselves, because they exchanged the truth about God for a lie and worshipped and served the creature rather than the Creator, who is blessed forever! Amen" (Romans 1:18-25).

God's Truth is revealed in nature. It cannot be denied. Wooden idols have been exchanged for gods of $$$$, sexual perversion, extravagance, and immoral "rights," and the wicked still try to suppress Truth and glorify lies, but there is no excuse for them, because God has embedded his Law in every heart and the gift of conscience in every soul. Those who choose to deny God must override their consciences to reconcile their evil choices. They clearly opt to follow Satan. The sides are chosen. Up for grabs are children and uninformed souls looking for Truth.

Propaganda

Propaganda is a powerful weapon of war. By definition, propaganda is biased toward one view or another, and whether it comes in the form of information, promises, or threats, it can modify the behavior of the populace. People or groups who want to manipulate public opinion generate propaganda. Propaganda differs from Truth in that Truth comes from God, who is Truth, and cannot be disputed. Satan uses propaganda to turn humankind away from the Truth. To use propaganda most effectively, it is best to start with young minds and teach them biased information as truth. This worked quite effectively in Nazi Germany where the government required that children be trained in Hitler's propaganda. Consider some of the propaganda our children are exposed to today:

Superheroes: Children are very attracted to superheroes and spend a great deal of time and energy with superhero books, TV shows and movies, video games, trading cards, and action figures. Superheroes have back-stories filled with psychological angst and rely on their own power to save the world. They perform superhuman feats and the thanks and glory goes to them. The superhero mystique teaches children an unrealistic self-reliance and a vengeful sense of justice. Children should be taught that **Jesus is the true superhero!** He really exists, has every real super power, died for us and came back to life! He is immortal, walked through walls, and appeared and disappeared at will! What more could people want? Leaping tall buildings? He created the raw materials to construct the building from nothing, gave intellect to the designers, and talent to the craftsmen. Not only that, Jesus comes to save each and every one of us personally. But in popular culture, Jesus is not presented to children as a superhero. Children are more likely to be exposed to his name used in a curse!

Corruption: Innocent hearts are assailed by entertainment and advertising industries that glorify sin, violence and revenge, and heroes that save the world wearing G-strings. The sad results? Children are doing what children do; they are imitating the sinful, violent, and sexual behavior. This type of propaganda steals the joy of innocence from children who are being taught a lie–that these perversions are normal and acceptable.

Un-truth: Our children are bombarded with propaganda to insure the continuation of human folly. They are denied knowledge of God's Truth and indoctrinated with distorted values in God-free school systems. Truth is objective. It is revealed in the order of God's creation and can be found through faith and reason. When God's Truth is denied, humankind suffers from moral disorder.

Order cannot exist without reasonable guidelines. What happens in a big city when the traffic lights go out? Chaos reigns and no one makes progress. To restore order lost by the rejection of God's Truth, leaders make more laws; but justice cannot be legislated by a society that rejects the basis of all justice: God. God is Truth. All justice stems from Truth. Many lawmakers say they believe in God, but Truth demands that they obey God's commandments to receive his wisdom.

Truth cannot be taught without mentioning the only source of Truth: God. Without God, what are our schools and universities teaching? There is no wisdom without God. Intellect without wisdom is dangerous as evidenced by the resulting decay of virtue and values. Intellect gives the means; wisdom supplies the meaning. In other words, just because we are intelligent enough to do something does not mean it is the intelligent thing to do.

How did this happen!? The insidious perversion of the Truth. How else could children's prayers in schools and public places be outlawed under the pretext of freedom of religion? We are being robbed of our God-given right to openly and freely live our faith as we strive for eternal life!

Look and see! Leaders from presidents to principals who are entrusted with our well-being and our children's futures are institutionalizing sin! Sitting back and watching the destruction of our youth and Christian institutions is inexcusable! Make known your outrage at the violence being done to innocent souls. What did Jesus do? Jesus expressed his outrage very clearly and opposed the leaders who perverted God's Truth to further their agendas.[29] Follow him!

God's Abundant Communication

In war, the first strategy of the enemy is to cut off its adversaries' lines of communication, and make no mistake—Satan is our enemy and we are at war! Satan tries to convince us that prayer is a waste of time, or that God is not listening and we are on our own. Satan wants us to be careless and ignorant of God's Will, so he distracts us with unnecessary busyness. He does not want us to think about God, read his Word, or pray. But, if we make time, put God first, lay aside the distractions for a while, and pray, communicate with God and discern his Will, we can destroy Satan's battle tactics and supply of ammunition: his lies.

God has offered us his friendship, eternal joy, and perfect happiness. Communication (prayer) is the key. So, just how do we go about communicating with God? This may surprise you, but God is very accessible. From our creation, God has spoken with humankind. What does the Bible record about God's personal relationships with human beings? Let's start at the beginning:

God spoke to Adam and Eve and cared for them even after they sinned.

When God showed Abel that he was pleased with his offerings, his brother, Cain, became jealous. "The Lord said to Cain, 'Why are you angry, and why has your countenance fallen? If you do well, will you not be accepted? And if you do not do well, sin is lurking at the door; its desire is for you, but you must master it'" (Genesis 4:6-7). In his mercy, God warned Cain against his jealous anger, but Cain would not listen. He did not master his jealousy and killed Abel.[30]

"Enoch walked with God; then he was no more, because God took him" (Genesis 5:24). Genesis records that the all the patriarchs died except Enoch, but that "God took him."

Do not forget God's conversations with Noah and Abraham.

God sent his angel to speak to Hagar, the servant of Sarah, to comfort her after Abraham sent her and their son Ishmael out into the desert. Desperate after their water ran out, she placed Ishmael under a bush. "Then she went and sat down opposite him a good way off, about the distance of a bowshot; for she said, 'Do not let me look on the death of the child.' And as she sat opposite him, she lifted up her voice and wept. And God heard the voice of the boy; and the angel of God called to Hagar from heaven, and said to her, 'What troubles you, Hagar? Do not be afraid; for God has heard the voice of the boy where he is. Come, lift up the boy and hold him fast with your hand, for I will make a great nation of him'" (Genesis 21:16-18).

Abraham sent a faithful servant to find a wife for Isaac. The faithful servant stopped at the well in Nahor and prayed for a sign to help him recognize the woman God had chosen for Isaac. He prayed that she would offer him water and draw water for his camels. "Before he had finished speaking, there was Rebekah, who was born to Bethuel son of Milcah, the wife of Nahor, Abraham's brother, coming out with her water jar on her shoulder" (Genesis 24:15). Rebekah offered water to the faithful servant and drew water for his camels. Rebekah became Isaac's wife and the mother of Esau and Jacob.

God spoke to Moses and his brother, Aaron (Exodus, Leviticus, Numbers, and Deuteronomy). Then God spoke to Joshua, instructed him to follow the Law of Moses, and promised to be with him as he led God's people into the Promised Land. See Joshua 1:1-9.

God spoke to his people through his Judges. Following God's instructions, Deborah guided Barak to seize Mount Tabor. At Barak's request, she even went with him to war. See Judges 4:4-9.

When Israel was being oppressed by Midian, God commissioned Gideon to defeat the Midianites. See Judges 6-7.

God's angel spoke to the barren wife of Manoah and told her that she would have a son, and repeated the promise to her husband. Their child was Samson, as in Samson and Delilah. See Judges 13:2-24.

God spoke through Old Testament prophets, who he called to speak his words to the Israelite people. There are well-known prophets, who have books of the Bible named after them, as well as many unnamed prophets who spoke God's words.

God also spoke directly to the kings of Judah and Israel. Some, like David and Solomon, listened to God. Some kings refused to listen to God, like Manasseh, who built altars to the Baals. "The Lord spoke to Manasseh and to his people, but they gave no heed" (2 Chronicles 33:10). Manasseh ended up a prisoner in Babylon but, "While he was in distress he entreated the favor of the Lord his God and humbled himself greatly before the God of his ancestors. He prayed to him, and God received his entreaty, heard his plea, and restored him again to Jerusalem and to his kingdom. Then Manasseh knew that the Lord indeed was God" (2 Chronicles 33:12-13).

Then Jesus came and announced the Kingdom of God. Jesus spoke to all the people who gathered to listen, both those who loved to hear his words and those who would turn his words against him.

Do you think Jesus stopped speaking to his people after he ascended into heaven? Not a chance!

He spoke to Saul in a bright light that temporarily blinded him on the road to Damascus. Saul was Jesus' enemy until that moment. Saul (a.k.a. Paul) told his conversion story many times, as he spread the Gospel throughout the Roman Empire. Numerous conversions resulted, and it all started when Jesus spoke to Paul and Paul listened. See Acts 9:1-9.

After Paul's conversion, the Lord told Ananias to go lay hands on Paul so that he might see again. After reminding God that Paul was an avid persecutor of Christians, Ananias obeyed. Paul received the Holy Spirit and regained his vision. The many Gentile conversions that resulted from Paul's ministry depended upon one man, Ananias, taking a risk to do God's Will. See Acts 9:10-19.

The Holy Spirit told Philip to join an Ethiopian court official who was on his way home after worshiping in Jerusalem. Philip explained scripture to him and he asked to be baptized. The court official returned home rejoicing and ready to spread the good news about Jesus in Ethiopia. See Acts 8:26-39.

God communicates with his people in ways unique to each one and the work he gives them. God sent an angel to the Virgin Mary and spoke to Joseph in a dream. The three wise men were drawn to the birth of Jesus in Bethlehem by prophesy and a star. The same event was announced to the shepherds by angels. God's communication is uniquely personal and intimate.

These are just a few examples of people in the Bible who responded to God's invitation. We cannot know how many people told God "No." We always have the freedom to refuse God's Will. But, "...to whom can we go?" (John 6:68)

It's Time for a Story

Pat was having a rough morning, and feeling exasperated, shouted out loud, "Lord, I need a friend!" There came an answer! "*I am* your friend." Shocked, Pat knew instantly who had spoken and blurted out, "But you are Jesus!" The conversation continued:

Jesus: "*I am* your friend."

Pat: "But I want a human friend. I can't just sit and chat with you, or go for coffee..."

Jesus: "We are chatting now and you are drinking coffee, and I was born as truly human as you. By the way, I like the way Shari cut your hair."

Pat: "See! How can I go to Shari and tell her that Jesus likes my haircut?"

Jesus: "Just tell Shari that I love her."

Pat: "Lord, you know everything. I need someone I can tell my problems to."

Jesus: "Don't you want to take your problems to someone who can help you find answers?"

Pat: "That's cool. You will solve my problems!"

Jesus: "No, I will *help you* solve your problems. I gave you the gift of free will so you can make your own choices. Life is not as simple as good or bad choices, but about how all of the choices you make weave into a tapestry that is your life. Each choice is important just as each stitch in the tapestry is important."

Pat: "What about bad choices?"

Jesus: "Look at the bad choices as learning the hard way. If it is a sinful choice, repent, learn, and move on."

Pat: "A friend would never talk to me about sin."

Jesus: "Is that honest? Objectively speaking, sin is very popular. Why would you and your friends avoid the subject?"

Pat: "Come to think about it, we wouldn't avoid the subject, but we would talk about other people's sins, the ones we see in the news."

Jesus: "Don't get me started on the news! A ubiquitous process of gathering rumor and innuendo and presenting it as fact! It has done a lot of damage to the innocent."

Pat: "What do you mean, ubiquitous?"

Jesus: "There are no rules. People gather the information they choose and distort it into a story that mirrors their own ideology. Human beings, on their own, cannot be objective. All human decisions reflect personal attitudes and knowledge. Humankind, without my help, has no point of reference to be objective. Those with the responsibility to provide news must pray and practice objectivity, and I will give them the gift of objectivity."

Pat: "Why don't you just give them the gift of objectivity?"

Jesus: "Not everyone wants or will accept my gifts. They turn my graces away. Those who want my gifts ask for them, and I give them what they need."

Pat: "Does that go for judges, too?"

Jesus: "Yes, no human being can be objective without prayer. That is why I told my disciples not to judge each other."

Pat: "But we have to have a criminal justice system!"

Jesus: "I am there. Do not despair. I can make good out of any evil."

Pat: "So you basically just go around picking up the pieces."

Jesus: "Unfortunately, that's the way it is these days. I wish my children would consult me first. They have my Word, and my Spirit dwells in them. It would save them a lot of trouble."

Pat: "I know I'm guilty. I'm sorry for ignoring your help."

Jesus: "Apology accepted. By the way, I'm proud of you for losing weight. Keep it up! You are improving your health."

Pat: "I prayed for your help and I know you are helping me; thank-you."

Jesus: "I just gave you a few inspirations to help you improve your diet. You chose to implement them. So, will you be my friend?"

Pat: "Yes, Lord. I see the advantage to being your friend."

Jesus: "Advantage! Oi vey! I love you, Pat. We can talk about advantages later."

Pat: "I love you, too. I mean, as much as I can. Good-bye."

Jesus: "Never good-bye. I am always with you."

CHAPTER 5

Lord, Teach Us to Pray

· ·

"Now when all the people were baptized, and when Jesus also had been baptized and was *praying*,[31] the heaven was opened, and the Holy Spirit descended upon him in bodily form like a dove. And a voice came from heaven, 'You are my Son, the Beloved; with you I am well pleased'" (Luke 3:21-22). Jesus prayed to our Father and our Father gave Jesus the testimony he needed to authenticate his mission as the Messiah, the Son of God.

Why Did Jesus, Who Is God and Man, Pray?

"But now more than ever the word about Jesus spread abroad; many crowds would gather to hear him and to be cured of their diseases. But he would withdraw to deserted places and *pray*" (Luke 5:15-16). Jesus needed to recharge his batteries. He needed to talk to our Father. He needed to pray.

Jesus prayed before he chose his apostles: "Now during those days he went out to the mountain to *pray*; and he spent the night in prayer to God. And when day came, he called his disciples and chose twelve of them, whom he also named apostles" (Luke 6:12-13).

Jesus fed five thousand people. "And taking the five loaves and the two fish, *he looked up to heaven, and blessed* and broke them, and gave them to the disciples to set before the crowd. And all ate and were filled. What was left over was gathered up, twelve baskets of broken pieces" (Luke 9:16-17). Jesus prayed for our Father's blessing on his work.

"Once when Jesus was *praying* alone, with only the disciples near him, he asked them, 'Who do the crowds say that I am?'" (Luke 9:18). Peter answered for the disciples, "…The Messiah of God" (Luke 9:20).

"… Jesus took with him Peter and John and James, and went up on the mountain to *pray*. And while he was praying, the appearance of his face changed, and his clothes became dazzling white" (Luke 9:28-29). In prayer, Jesus received graces for his disciples.

When the seventy disciples joyfully returned after Jesus sent them out to preach in the towns, Jesus prayed in thanksgiving: "At that same hour *Jesus rejoiced in the Holy Spirit* and said, 'I thank you, Father, Lord of heaven and earth, because you have hidden these things from the wise and the intelligent and have revealed them to infants; yes, Father, for such was your gracious will'" (Luke 10:21).

"He was *praying* in a certain place, and after he had finished, one of his disciples said to him, 'Lord, teach us to pray, as John (the Baptist) taught his disciples'" (Luke 11:1). Jesus taught them the "Our Father." He prayed as an example for us to follow.

"Then he withdrew from them about a stone's throw, knelt down, and *prayed*, 'Father, if you are willing, remove this cup from me; yet, not my will but yours be done'" (Luke 22:41-42). Thus, Jesus prayed for the strength to do our Father's Will on the Mount of Olives.

Hanging on the cross, Jesus prayed. "Then Jesus said, 'Father, forgive them; for they do not know what they are doing…'" (Luke 23:34), and "… My God, my God, why have you forsaken me?" (Mark 15:34).

And, at the last moment of his life, his prayer was one of trust in our Father: "Then Jesus, crying with a loud voice, said, 'Father, into your hands I commend my spirit.' Having said this, he breathed his last" (Luke 23:46).

"Let the same mind be in you that was in Christ Jesus, who, though he was in the form of God, did not regard equality with God as something to be exploited, but emptied himself, taking the form of a slave, being born in human likeness. And being found in human form, he humbled himself and became obedient to the point of death—even death on a cross" (Philippians 2:5-8).

If Jesus, who was without sin, humbled himself to pray so frequently, how much more necessary is it for us to pray? In prayer, we come to know God in his goodness, and gain more than an intellectual knowledge of how much he loves us. In prayer, we discover the gifts and talents God has given us for our happiness and the benefit of others. In prayer, we ask for spiritual guidance to make moral decisions. In prayer, we receive wisdom and learn the truth about love. In prayer, we thank God for his grace and the promise of eternal glory in heaven. In prayer, we receive insights to relieve anxiety and confusion. In prayer, we ask and, from our Father's hands, we receive good things and yes, through prayer, God gives us miracles. In prayer, we find peace. Thank God! Prayer brings about a longing to obey our Father's Will out of love, as Jesus did. By means of prayer, we grow closer to God, who guides us to his heavenly kingdom and eternal happiness.

The Prayer Jesus Taught Us

When his disciples asked him how to pray, Jesus taught them the "Our Father." The early Church Fathers have commented at great length on the "Our Father" and it is important to read their writings for they were closest to the apostles whom Jesus taught. For our purpose, we will take a simple look at the prayer Jesus taught us:

"…Our Father in heaven, hallowed be your name.

Your kingdom come.

Your will be done, on earth as it is in heaven.

Give us this day our daily bread.

And forgive us our debts, as we also have forgiven our debtors.

And do not bring us to the time of trial, but rescue us from the evil one."

(Matthew 6:9-13).

"Our Father"–Jesus did not say "my father" or "your father." In two words, Jesus describes his relationship with us as his brothers and sisters, and with God as our Father. Think of the dignity that is ours! Think of the obligation that we have toward each other! The address "Our Father" gives us an understanding of the way God sees us. We are all one family!

Our Father wants to give us a legacy like any loving father, but our inheritance is not an earthly one. We cannot hold it in our hands. Our legacy is a share in the kingdom of God. "But, as it is written, 'What no eye has seen, nor ear heard, nor the human heart conceived, what God has prepared for those who love him'" (1 Corinthians 2:9). Heaven is beyond our human comprehension because we are limited by what our senses can perceive. We can say "as beautiful as a flower" or "as vast as the sea" but flowers and the sea can only be recognized through our human senses. What heavenly things can we grasp with our worldly senses? "These things God has revealed to us through the Spirit; for the Spirit searches everything, even the depths of God. For what human being knows what is truly human except the human spirit that is within? So also no one comprehends what is truly God's except the Spirit of God. Now we have received not the spirit of the world, but the Spirit that is from God, so that we may understand the gifts bestowed on us by God. And we speak of these things in words not taught by human wisdom but taught by the Spirit, interpreting spiritual things to those who are spiritual. Those who are unspiritual do not receive the gifts of God's Spirit, for they (the gifts)[32] are foolish to them, and they are unable to understand them because they (the gifts of God's Spirit) are spiritually discerned." (1 Corinthians 2:10-14).

The key to knowing the things of God is a relationship with the Holy Spirit. Our Father has given us this great gift. To become spiritual people, we must do as Jesus did: be obedient to our Father, pray, and listen to the Holy Spirit teach us the wisdom of God.

"In heaven"–Jesus tells us that God our Father resides in a physical location, heaven, the place to where Jesus ascended after he rose from the dead. But Jesus also said, "…Those who love me will keep my word, and my Father will love them, and we will come to them and make our home with them" (John 14:23). Isn't heaven where God resides? So, it is also within our own souls! In addition to the heavens which Stephen saw open up to reveal "…the Son of Man standing at the right hand of God" (Acts 7:56), there is also the place where God makes his home within us, the light within our souls, God, who is everywhere and keeps all things in existence.

"Hallowed be your name"—What is our name but words that identify us? God's name is "hallowed" or holy because God is holy. God commanded his people to respect his holy name. It is simple logic. If we do not respect God, we most certainly will not respect each other, and damage is done to Christian unity. Why do people think it is acceptable to insult God? God said to Moses, "You shall not make wrongful use of the name of the Lord your God, for the Lord will not acquit anyone who misuses his name" (Exodus 20:7). Is our generation ever in trouble! Watch a movie or television or attend a sporting event and hear the number of times the name of Jesus is used as a careless expression of dissatisfaction or in a curse. If we belittle God, we belittle our own dignity as children of God. Freedom to speak as we please does not give us permission to abuse the dignity of other human beings. How much more do we owe the dignity of God? What are

we doing? Why do we promote disdain for our loving God by giving tacit support to his abusers?

Defend God's name against those who would misuse it, at home, at work, at school, everywhere! Our God is the Living God! He is our Father Almighty! Object when public figures, entertainers, or other people abuse God's name. How many times do you hear someone yell, "O Satan!" when things go wrong? That would be more appropriate than yelling, "O Jesus!" in anger. Say God's name reverently, as prayer. Nothing else is acceptable.

"Your kingdom come. Your will be done, on earth as it is in heaven."– Jesus taught us to pray for the coming of the Kingdom of God. We are not praying for some abstract idea. The coming of the Kingdom God promised is described in Revelations 21:1-4, "Then I saw a new heaven and a new earth; for the first heaven and the first earth had passed away, and the sea was no more. And I saw the holy city, the new Jerusalem, coming down out of heaven from God, prepared as a bride adorned for her husband. And I heard a loud voice from the throne saying, 'See, the home of God is among mortals. He will dwell with them; they will be his peoples, and God himself will be with them; he will wipe every tear from their eyes. Death will be no more; mourning and crying and pain will be no more, for the first things have passed away.'"

The children of God will dwell with God, full of knowledge, wisdom, and joy. The "inhabitants of the earth,"[33] those who choose to be unspiritual persons, freely reject the joy God offers. We pray that God's Will is done on earth so that we may soon enjoy the kingdom of love that is his Will.

"Give us this day our daily bread."–These words are a prayer for our needs day by day. Jesus did not teach us to ask for prosperity or a comfortable future, but only what we need each day. Trust that God will give us what we need. He sees the overall picture and does what is best for us.

When we ask for "our daily bread," our request is not limited to physical needs. We also need spiritual food. On the night before Jesus was crucified, while he was at supper with his apostles, "He said to them, 'I have eagerly desired to eat this Passover with you before I suffer; for I tell you, I will not eat it until it is fulfilled in the kingdom of God" (Luke 22:15-16). "Then he took the loaf of bread, and when he had given thanks, he broke it and gave it to them, saying, 'This is my body, which is given for you. Do this in remembrance of me.' And he did the same with the cup after supper, saying, 'This cup that is poured out for you is the new covenant in my blood'" (Luke 22:19-20). As sharing in the first Passover lamb united and defined the Israelites as children of God through the Covenant of Moses, so Christians, carrying out the command of Jesus to "Do this in remembrance of me," are united and defined in the Breaking of the Bread as the children of the New Covenant. Jesus feeds us with his Word and his Body and Blood so we may be transformed by his redeeming love and enter the kingdom of God.

"And forgive us our debts, as we have forgiven our debtors."–This concept is simple, yet we find many reasons to ignore it, usually beginning with the excuse that the other guy doesn't deserve our forgiveness. But Jesus says: "For if you forgive others their trespasses, your heavenly Father will also forgive you; but if you do not forgive others, neither will your Father forgive your trespasses" (Matthew 6:14-15). And, "Do not judge, so that you may not be judged. For with the judgment you make you will be judged, and the measure you give will be the measure you get" (Matthew 7:1-2). Paul instructs the Colossians: "As God's chosen ones, holy and beloved, clothe yourselves with compassion, kindness, humility, meekness, and patience. Bear with one another and, if anyone has a complaint against another, forgive each other; just as the Lord has forgiven you, so you also must forgive" (Colossians 3:12-13). No holding grudges and no revenge

planning allowed! "For judgment will be without mercy to anyone who has shown no mercy; mercy triumphs over judgment" (James 2:13).

"And do not bring us to the time of trial,"–It is proper to ask God for help. We are very imperfect. In fact, we have a bad habit of telling God what his Will is! Here we acknowledge our weakness and ask for the virtue of humility. Humility accepts God's grace, but arrogance thinks it needs no help. Only by humbly asking God to reduce our trials to manageable levels, and to give us the love, faith, and grace we need to persevere, can we hope to succeed as Christians. Only in humility can we learn to love the Will of God; and it must be with humility that we ask for rescue and guidance.

"But rescue us from the evil one."–This last line is not a prayer to avoid suffering on earth. That is not logical. Jesus suffered rejection and threats against his life at the hands of his enemies until he was finally crucified for doing our Father's Will. And he allowed his own mother, Mary, to suffer the sorrows of knowing Simeon's prophesy, "Then Simeon blessed them and said to his mother Mary, 'This child is destined for the falling and rising of many in Israel, and to be a sign that will be opposed so that the inner thoughts of many will be revealed—and a sword will pierce your own soul too'" (Luke 2:34-35). She knew the pain of witnessing Jesus' cruel death.[34] God could have protected Mary from the devastating grief, but she chose to remain close to her son to the last.

Jesus instructs us in this last line to ask for protection from the evil traps that the devil prepares for us. Sometimes an opportunity that looks good leads us on the wrong path. Like Eve, we look at the apple and it looks just fine, so we take that bite. Like Adam, someone we trust takes a bite of the apple, so why shouldn't we? "Rescue us from the evil one" is the prayer that asks for the wisdom to know if the apples we encounter lead us on the path to heaven or the road to hell. We pray for discernment and the courage to choose what is holy, for a good conscience, and the strength to endure temptation without compromising our souls.

Do not allow the busyness of your daily duties deprive you of the joy of meeting our Father in prayer. You are not absolutely indispensable at all times and the world will not end when you die. Someone else will be there to take over your tasks. Make time to enjoy the friendship of God. The rest of your time will become more productive. It is a good thing to have a working relationship with the God who will judge us as his friend, or not!

CHAPTER 6

The Beatitudes

• •

*J*esus gave us a set of instructions that we call the Beatitudes. We have dutifully memorized them, but do we truly understand the Beatitudes as the blueprint of how we are expected to live .as Christians? As we read them here, let us ask the Holy Spirit to enlighten us and increase our understanding of Jesus' teachings.

The Beatitudes are virtues to acquire and their corresponding rewards. For example, "Blessed are the poor in spirit, for theirs is the kingdom of heaven" (Matthew 5:3) gives us a goal, "the kingdom of heaven," and the way to get there, becoming "poor in spirit." The Beatitudes require action but are also states of being. In other words, achieving the virtue "poor in spirit" requires both practicing "poor in spirit" and desiring to be "poor in spirit." The practicing and the desiring, through the grace of God, will engender the actions in our souls that make us truly be "poor in spirit."

Immediately after teaching the Beatitudes to his disciples, Jesus tells them, "You are the salt of the earth; but if salt has lost its taste, how can its saltiness be restored? It is no longer good for anything, but is thrown out and trampled underfoot. You are the light of the world. A city built on a hill cannot be hid. No one after lighting a lamp puts it under the bushel basket, but on the lampstand, and it gives light to all in the house. In the same way, let your light shine before others, so that they may see your good works and give glory to your Father in heaven" (Matthew 5:13-16). Some argue that if we have faith that Jesus died to take away our sins and we acknowledge his resurrection, we are righteous and no further action is required on our part. People cannot simply call themselves Christian; they must do Christian, that is, be like Christ, and Jesus was a doer. "But be doers of the word, and not merely hearers who deceive themselves. For if any are hearers of the word and not doers, they are like those who look at themselves in a mirror; for they look at themselves and, on going away, immediately forget what they were like. But those who look into the perfect law, the law of liberty, and persevere, being not hearers who forget but doers who act—they will be blessed in their doing" (James 1:22-25). And, "What good is it, my brothers and sisters, if you say you have faith but do not have works? Can faith save you? If a brother or sister is naked and lacks daily food, and one of you says to them, 'Go in peace; keep warm and eat your fill,' and yet you do not supply their bodily needs, what is the good of that? So faith by itself, if it has no works, is dead. But someone will say, 'You have faith, and I have works.' Show me your faith apart from your works, and I by my works will show you my faith" (James 2:14-18).

As we read the Beatitudes, keep in mind that they require action. The Beatitudes according to Matthew 5:3-11 are:

"Blessed are the poor in spirit, for theirs is the kingdom of heaven.

Blessed are those who mourn, for they will be comforted.

Blessed are the meek, for they will inherit the earth.

Blessed are those who hunger and thirst for righteousness, for they will be filled.

Blessed are the merciful, for they will receive mercy.

Blessed are the pure in heart, for they will see God.

Blessed are the peacemakers, for they will be called children of God.

Blessed are those who are persecuted for righteousness' sake, for theirs is the kingdom of heaven.

Blessed are you when people revile you and persecute you and utter all kinds of evil against you falsely on my account. Rejoice and be glad, for your reward is great in heaven, for in the same way they persecuted the prophets who were before you."

"Blessed are the poor in spirit, for theirs is the kingdom of heaven."

Someone said that "poor in spirit" means the liquor is running out. Irreverent, perhaps, but the truth is "poor in spirit" is poorly understood. Jesus is the best example of what it means to be poor in spirit. Not only was he financially poor—his first crib was an animal's feeding trough, a situation which has been highly romanticized but in reality was cold and unpleasant—but he made no effort to accumulate earthly goods. Jesus' focus was on the work his Father had given him to do. He kept only what he needed. Jesus was an itinerant teacher. Carrying around an accumulation of things would have interfered with his work of spreading the gospel.

The poor in spirit focus on the work God has given them to do. They have confidence in God. They do not tell God what they need. They simply ask with the certitude that no matter what happens, God will turn it into good. The qualities of the poor in spirit are trust in God's love, and gratitude for everything as a gift from him. Those who are truly poor in spirit have peaceful spirits. This does not mean they are unemotional. Tears are a powerful weapon in God's army, and joy and laughter give the strength to fight on. But the hope, that comes from faith in God's love and trust that he is working for the good of all, gives a deep sense of spiritual peace.

It is not impossible to be poor in spirit and wealthy but the distractions caused by having wealth can make keeping God's Will in perspective more difficult. For example, faithful Christian Joe lands a well-paying job and is appropriately grateful to God. He has faith that God has a purpose for this grace; that's easy. But once the money is in hand, complications arise. It is more difficult to be poor in spirit when worldly distractions get in our way.

Look at Joe. He now has a good job and life is great. He falls into thinking he can take care of himself. Temptation to a disordered self-reliance is overwhelming. After all, he can buy anything he wants so he does not have to ask God for what he needs. He forgets to thank God for his blessings. Poverty in spirit loses its attraction. Then Joe's company begins laying-off personnel. Joe worries that he will lose his comfortable lifestyle. He compromises his Christian values to keep his job. Unnerved by the near loss of his job he grows afraid that his money will be spent too quickly; that he will lose his retirement; that he will not be able to afford his vacation, etc. Anxiety becomes greed. Greed becomes an infection. What happened to trusting God and focusing on his purpose?! See how easily Joe fell into foolishness! See how easy it was for him to spiral away from his good intentions. The moral of the story? Losing focus on God's Will is perilous for the soul.

Sometimes, being poor in spirit requires denying our own desires and we suffer. We cannot fathom God's reasons, but God has a purpose and he allows no suffering to go to waste. It is when we hold on to our faith and hope while we are suffering that our prayers are most powerful. Remember that Jesus suffered and died to redeem us. His focus was on our Father's Will, redeeming humankind, and giving us an example to follow. We cannot follow Jesus more closely than when we are suffering. Trust in God even when, in the darkness of suffering, we cannot understand his purpose. Complete trust in God defines poor in spirit.

The Beatitudes Are One Instruction

The Beatitudes are to be understood as one instruction, not individual orders. Do not think you can 'do' poor in spirit and not 'do' merciful. To the truly poor in spirit, mercy comes naturally. The poor in spirit recognize what they are and what they are not. They know they are not perfect and humbly acknowledge the wisdom of God by accepting the standards of behavior that he impressed upon all souls, the natural order, and his revelations in Scripture.

The merciful quite naturally work for justice for all people. They see compassion as paramount. If none of us is perfect, then it is only logical that we deal with each other's weaknesses mercifully or waste all of our energy fighting. The merciful hunger and thirst for righteousness, which is the justice that comes from God. They naturally want to work to against evil in the world. Mother Teresa of Calcutta, Martin Luther King, Jr., and Father Damian, who lived and worked with lepers, are all people who changed the world by fighting the injustice they saw. They spent their lives working for God's justice and practiced the mercy they themselves desired.

"Blessed are those who mourn, for they will be comforted."

Mourning was not in the original design of human nature. When they were created, Adam and Eve had no need to mourn. Mourning came into the world as a result of sin and now mourning is proper and natural for all human beings. Mourning brings with it a range of human emotions: disbelief, anger, sadness, and depression. We mourn for lost loved ones. We mourn because of lost expectations and heartbreaking disappointments. We mourn when our friends move away, and when we see our loved ones do foolish things that will cause them pain.

Mourning is painful, but with mourning comes the promise of God's comfort. He might send a person to comfort us, or a memory, or the perfect word to give us peace. And God gives us hope, hope of seeing our loved ones again, and hope of final justice. We mourn because we love. Mourning drives out that core selfishness that causes us to be unkind to others. It teaches us compassion and humility, and it makes us know how much we need each other. We may not see positive changes right away. It takes time. Meanwhile, as mourning reshapes our hearts, we will be comforted.

While mourning is appropriate in many situations, there are people who go through all of the stages of mourning because their car is scratched. How can someone whose priorities are so out of whack be comforted? Even God can't comfort them. They won't let him!

"Blessed are the meek, for they will inherit the earth."

Synonyms for meek include humility and modesty, but also timidity and submissiveness. In our culture the word "meek" has a negative connotation. Is it any wonder we find this Beatitude confusing? To understand the meek of this Beatitude, we must look at Jesus. He was a charismatic man with the power to attract great crowds. People longed for the truth in his words. Jesus courageously confronted powerful religious and political authorities, challenging their hypocrisy. He wandered the countryside for three years with few physical comforts, depending upon the charity of those who listened to his message for food and shelter. Jesus was tired, hungry, and thirsty, but still he pressed on to Jerusalem knowing exactly what awaited him there. When the time came to confront the horrifying reality of his execution, knowing the tortures he was about to endure, Jesus waited in the Garden of Olives for Judas, his betrayer. What is so meek about Jesus' life? Jesus did the Will of his Father in heaven. To do the "meek" of the

Beatitudes, we must have the courage to accept the Will of God, even when we do not want it. We must pray as Jesus prayed, listen to our Father as Jesus did, and then we must act upon the inspirations of the Holy Spirit.

Look at the disciples who followed Jesus. They were willing to accept torture and death rather than worship pagan gods or submit to laws that violated the teachings of Jesus. These, our forebears in Christianity, were neither timid nor submissive. They had humility and modesty, accepting that they were not an end in themselves. They were part of God's greater plan, and they took comfort in that truth. The meek give their free wills in a spirit of cooperation with God's Will out of love for him and for their neighbor. What amazing courage it takes to be meek in God's army!

"Blessed are those who hunger and thirst for righteousness"

We know what powerful drives hunger and thirst are. Location and lack or abundance of food and water have driven mass migrations and shaped nations. The potato famine in Ireland changed the populations of both Ireland and the United States. Starvation has been used as an effective tool of war to control and to oppress populations from ancient times to this very day. Hunger and thirst threaten our basic survival. Yet hunger and thirst are the words Jesus used, words that speak to the core of our existence. Is the human need for righteousness, variously defined as honesty, decency, morality, virtue, and God's justice, the same type of strong and all-consuming basic human need? Is it as important as the need for food? A look at human history gives us the answer, a resounding "Yes!" Indeed, without the basics of decency, morality, virtue and true justice that come from God, we are less than human.

Examples of humankind's passion for righteousness are everywhere. Those who suffer indignity in this world, and those who are driven to do something about others' sufferings, all hunger and thirst for God's righteousness. Deep within our human essence, we long for a just world where all can know God's peace, and the driving force is love. Jesus said, "This is my commandment, that you love one another as I have loved you" (John 15:12). Love is the reason we work to achieve righteousness in our families, communities, and countries. Jesus gives us the assurance that we will not be disappointed. We will be filled.

"Blessed are the merciful, for they will receive mercy."

Blessed are we when we can feel compassion for others, for we know that God's love is in our hearts. We know we are alive and still human. This world is a difficult place. Christians are charged with making life more compassionate.

This Beatitude is so important that it is also part of the prayer Jesus taught us, the "Our Father." Jesus makes it very clear that the degree of mercy we have shown to others will determine the degree of mercy God shows us. So why do we refuse to forgive each other? Consider the consequences of holding that grudge. Are we absolutely sure that our thoughts, words, and actions are so perfect that we can take the risk of being forgiven by God the way we forgive others? Jesus does not ask the impossible of us. If he asks us to forgive each other, he will give us the grace to do it. Each of us has hurt someone. The degree of hurt is often subjective; we cannot know the hearts and minds of those around us. We seem more capable of injustice than compassion and mercy. Because this is true of all humanity, God requires us to show mercy to one another.

Jesus disciples were not inclined to seek out Saul/Paul and forgive him, but God had a great plan for Paul that required just that. Unless we have more insight than the disciples who knew Jesus, we would be unwise to judge each other harshly. It is foolish not to take advantage of Jesus' offer, "Blessed are the merciful, for they will receive mercy."

"Blessed are the pure in heart, for they will see God."

Being "pure in heart" begins with the desire to please God in all we do. Often this desire to please God is awakened after years of trying to do our own wills and suffering the consequences. Once we realize that we have made our lives miserable, we begin to look for a better way, and lo and behold, there it is—God's Will. It has always been there, in front of us, but our hearts were so cluttered by self-love, love for stuff and doing our own thing, that we did not see it. God's Will is so simple. He wants us to love him and join him in heaven.

God can make his home in pure hearts without having to compete with silly distractions. The more we learn to prioritize, that is, assign appropriate degrees of importance to everything in our lives, the more room for love, for God. We must start from where we are. Right now, on our scale of 1-10, football games may be a 10 and God a 7. It helps us to prioritize if we think about what lasts forever and what does not. The closer God gets to 10 the more our hearts will grow and expand in love.

The pure in heart see all things as gifts from God. They help other people see God by sharing God's love. To be pure in heart, we must make loving God our first priority, love our neighbor, make the effort to simplify our lives, shed our stuff and our self-love to make room for the truly important and everlasting, and God will do the rest.

"Blessed are the peacemakers, for they will be called children of God."

Why are peacemakers called "children of God?" Because the only true peace is given by God. Jesus said, "Peace I leave with you; my peace I give to you. I do not give to you as the world gives. Do not let your hearts be troubled, and do not let them be afraid" (John 14:27).

Peace in this world? Not since Adam and Eve ate the apple! However, Christians can have peace in this world, the peace that Christ gives when we live our faith and trust that God helps us, protects us, and guides us to heaven, which is the point and purpose of our lives. And Christ's peace is contagious. Peacemakers make everyone around them feel more peaceful. Peacemakers keep their souls calm and pay attention to the promptings of the Holy Spirit. They are careful not to lose their own peace by foolishness. Peacemakers are children of God because they listen to God.

Some peacemakers are diplomats entrusted with the responsibility of ending wars, but few of us will ever have the opportunity to promote peace on a grand scale. But we are all called to keep peace each day in our own lives by controlling our anger and irritation over trivial matters. For example, your friend walks by and makes no acknowledgement, not even a smile. You can choose to be angry and tell everyone your friend is rude and spread ill feelings, or you can choose to be a peacemaker and ignore the slight. Perhaps your friend was preoccupied and did not see you. Are you really so important that you must be acknowledged every time a friend passes by? If your friend lacks charity, then what good will come of being angry with her? What she needs is an example of charity. Do not make up motives in your mind for other people's behavior. It takes away your peace because no one can fully understand another person's motives. Stop the dialogue in your mind! Practice charity! Practice forgiveness! Refuse to give up your own peace.

Every Christian can be a peacemaker. Keep guard over your thoughts. Question them. Say to yourself: "Why am I thinking this? Is this something I should be concerned about? Is this a situation I should act upon? Can I be helpful? Are my thoughts charitable and kind or am I judging unjustly?" When we judge the hearts and motives of others, we are trying to be God! Stop trying to be God and become children of God. "Bless those who persecute you; bless and do not curse them. Rejoice with those who rejoice, weep with those who weep. Live in harmony with one another; do not be haughty, but associate with the lowly; do not claim to be wiser than you are. Do not repay anyone evil for evil, but take thought for what is noble in the sight of all. If it is possible, so far as it depends on you, live peaceably with all. Beloved, never avenge yourselves, but leave room for the wrath of God; for it is written, 'Vengeance is mine, I will repay, says the Lord.' No, 'if your enemies are hungry, feed them; if they are thirsty, give them something to drink; for by doing this you will heap burning coals on their heads.' Do not be overcome by evil, but overcome evil with good" (Romans 12: 14-21). Left to ourselves, we can only fail these instructions miserably, but in God's grace, we can be peacemakers and children of God.

"Blessed are those who are persecuted for righteousness' sake for theirs is the kingdom of heaven."

"Do not be conformed to this world, but be transformed by the renewing of your minds, so that you may discern what is the will of God—what is good and acceptable and perfect" (Romans 12:2). You can bet that if we are not "conformed to this world," our lives will be uncomfortable!

The abortion pill is legal and pharmacists have lost their jobs for refusing to dispense it. They are not "conformed to this world." Businesses and religious groups that risk destructive fines and financial ruin because they refuse to accept government mandates that violate God's Law are not "conformed to this world." Government workers who refuse to enforce immoral laws, and company employees who challenge the morality of greedy business practices and lose their livelihoods are not "conformed to this world." God is deeply offended. His beloved children are being persecuted for discerning and living his Will. Since they are no longer "conformed to this world," theirs is the kingdom of heaven. People, business entities, and countries that "conform to this world" subvert the freedom God gives to his children. They are doing the work of the father of lies, the devil. There is no room for them in God's Kingdom.

"Blessed are you when people revile you and persecute you and utter all kinds of evil against you falsely on my account."

"Rejoice and be glad, for your reward is great in heaven, for in the same way they persecuted the prophets who were before you" (Matthew 5:12). Is Jesus telling us that if we follow him and do as he did, we will be persecuted? Yes, that is exactly what he is saying. Remember the way God chose to redeem us. Jesus did not come to us with displays of wealth and grandeur and say, "I am God. Worship me." He was born a helpless baby, grew up as children grow, learned a trade, and worked for a living. When the time came to proclaim the gospel, Jesus enlisted the aid of disciples, gave them power over demons and power to heal, and sent them out to proclaim the kingdom of God. Everyday folks shared what Jesus had done for them with their families and friends. A true grass roots movement was formed.

Jesus did not mean to accomplish the redemption of the human race without our help. Of course, we are redeemed by the death of Jesus on the cross, but the spreading of the Word is left to us. In his death and resurrection, Jesus gave innumerable gifts to humanity, including the knowledge of God's infinite love for us, and the certainty that, through Jesus, we can be with God in heaven. Sharing the joy of God's love is our responsibility. Jesus left this responsibility with the apostles, disciples, holy women, and us, the Christians who come after.

Sometimes Christians find themselves maligned. But Jesus, who harmed no one, was crucified. Why? The answer is simple: his very existence. He made the authorities of the day uncomfortable because he condemned their hypocrisy. He spoke the Truth to people who did not want to hear the Truth. Jesus did not associate very much with the wealthy and powerful and, when he did, he was not treated with respect. Christians cannot expect to be treated better than Jesus. But do not lose heart. We are never alone in our efforts. Keep faith in Jesus' words, "your reward in heaven is great."

Christians, who live the Beatitudes, take risks. They work for justice, no matter where God's grace leads them. They promote the gospel of Jesus without uttering a word because their gentleness and peace are attractive to others. In a culture of advertising that promotes personal success based on everything but God, Christians demonstrate that the source of all success is God. In a society that places great value on amusements, Christians own the certainty that there is far more to life than enjoying the amusements this world has to offer. Most amusements are not evil, but as a steady diet, they are very unfulfilling. The world may think Christians are weird, especially when they invest their wealth and energy in helping people rather than making more money. I have made both types of investments and have received far more satisfying returns from investing in the futures of human beings than investing in financial markets. After all, futures in heaven are guaranteed not to decline!

CHAPTER 7

The Ten Commandments

. . . .

"All who obey his commandments abide in him, and he abides in them. And by this we know that he abides in us, by the Spirit that he has given us" (1 John 3:24).

The Ten Commandments are written in stone by God's own hand and are as important to us today as they were to the Israelites when God gave them to Moses. Thousands of years after Moses, Jesus told his followers: "... If you wish to enter into life, keep the commandments" (Matthew 19:17). "Keep" means more than obey. "Keep" means "not to swerve from or violate" and "to preserve or maintain" for the future (William Allan Neilson). Keeping the Ten Commandments helps us keep order in our lives and avoid sin.

What is sin? As defined in Webster's New International Dictionary of the English Language, Second Edition, Unabridged, sin is a "transgression of the law of God; disobedience to the Divine Will," and "failure to do as one ought toward one's fellow men" (William Allan Neilson). We are all sinners. We disregard the Divine Will and fail our neighbor from time to time. We all know the guilt and misery caused by sin. God our Father gave us the Ten Commandments to guide us to peace and happiness.

The Ten Commandments puts into plain words the natural order of God's creation. God summarized the natural order on a simple stone instruction tablet for our good—not for his—so that we can live in peace. When we defy the natural order, we inflict chaos, conflict, corruption, and disillusionment upon ourselves. But nowadays, God's natural order is being supplanted by a perverted ideology that accepts all beliefs as truth. How can there be order in society when different groups insist upon imposing their contradictory "truths" upon the populace? What confusion! Who is qualified to help humankind keep order if not God who created us? Who makes the rules? Judges? Politicians? Special interest groups? Corporations? World bankers? Institutions? Individuals? Each of these groups imposes their own self-interested laws when God's Ten Commandments are pushed aside. The result is anarchy, persecution, chaos, and slavery. Without God's Law, disordered behavior and opinion is popularized and taught to children as truth, thereby infecting them. You can see where this is going…

The Great Corruption

God's definition of love is written in the Ten Commandments and exemplified by Jesus Christ. Corruptors of God's Truth justify their beliefs and actions by reasoning, "If God is love then all forms of love are from God." Their corrupt definition of love is: "If it feels good and it appears to be good to the populace, then it is good"—justification in numbers, not in Truth. This is the Great Corruption.

Here are a few points of enlightenment regarding the workings of the Great Corruption:

First, corruptors come up with an idea: a woman should not have to bear a child she does not want. She should have the freedom to solve her problem. The corruptors change an unborn child into a "problem" and killing the child into "freedom" with their rhetoric. However, God's commandments of love are now inconvenient since they forbid murder.

Secondly, corruptors announce this "freedom" in a way that makes it sound good. Their reasoning is, "If God is love then a loving God would not want a woman to suffer bearing a child she does not want." Their arguments are loud, repetitive, and full of faulty logic. The unborn child is labeled a "fetus," which is the unborn offspring of any vertebrate, placing unborn human babies in the same category as calves and piglets to dehumanize them. The human soul is an awkward reality that the distorters play down or deny, replacing God's natural order with perverted rhetoric. Even though the rhetoric is illogical, the populace listens because the corruptors are aggressive and unrelenting in their lies. The populace believes the corruptors' claims that abortion is a good way to be sympathetic toward a woman who does not want the child she has conceived. God's natural order is mocked and compassionate options that oppose the rhetoric of the corruptors are summarily excluded from public discussion.

Thirdly, enough of the populace is captivated by the Great Corruption that God's commandments are overridden by public opinion. However, individuals must still wrestle with their inner voices, the consciences that God gives to all people to help them know right from wrong. Opposing God's natural order, inherent in the Ten Commandments, is an uncomfortable feeling for all but the darkest souls.

Resolution: If the distorted position makes the populace uncomfortable, it cannot be the populace's fault. By their numbers, the populace has justified its opinion. Their discomfort must be the fault of Christians who follow God's commandments and will not yield to the Great Corruption. The populace justifies its position in this instance by attacking Christians as manipulative, uncharitable, and unjust in opposing women's freedom, when the opposite, which is a profound recognition and loving respect for the physical, psychological, intellectual, and spiritual dignity of women, is the Truth.

The Great Corruption has been used to justify all kinds of arrogant offenses against God's commandments. When will people ever understand that God established humankind on earth not for its own glory, but for the glory of God? We are created by God and can only reflect God's glory. We have nothing of our own: no glory, no wisdom, and no merit. We create nothing! Only by accepting this Truth, can we live with each other in peace and enjoy the divinely ordained fulfillment of our lives. We are held in existence at every moment by God's love! How arrogant are the distorters who deny the natural order reflected in God's commandments!

Before we review the Ten Commandments, a few considerations:

Accept the Ten Commandments as they truly are, an expression of God's love for us, and commit to them as the Law Jesus instructed us to live by. The charity inherent in the Ten Commandments brings God's peace, to both individuals and the societies that honor them. This explains why societies that teach their children to disobey and even mock God's Laws are so angry and violent.

Secondly, the Ten Commandments are good for examining our lives in prayer to help us work toward living as Jesus taught. We must examine our own personal obedience to God's Law. It is tempting to be sidetracked and examine our wife's or husband's, parents', neighbors', co-workers', etcetera's sins, but then, we defeat the purpose. We must each look at our own successes, failures, and lukewarmness in light of the Ten Commandments.

Thirdly, this "examination" is not a pass/fail test. It is a "What can I do to cooperate with God's Will and increase my love for God and neighbor?' review of our lives. Ask God to open your heart to understand his love and purpose inherent in the Ten Commandments.

These are the Ten Commandments as set down in Exodus 20:1-17:

How to Love God

"...I am the Lord your God..." (Exodus 20:2). "Then God spoke all these words: I am the Lord your God, who brought you out of the land of Egypt, out of the house of slavery; you shall have no other gods before me. You shall not make for yourself an idol, whether in the form of anything that is in heaven above, or that is on the earth beneath, or that is in the water under the earth. You shall not bow down to them or worship them; for I the Lord your God am a jealous God, punishing children for the iniquity of parents, to the third and the fourth generation of those who reject me, but showing steadfast love to the thousandth generation of those who love me and keep my commandments" (Exodus 20:1-6).

"...you shall have no other gods before me" (Exodus 20:3). Any concept, desire, object, or person that directs our attention away from God is a false god, no matter how good and right it might seem. We live for God and eternal life is found only in him. This commandment tells us to keep our focus on him.

Jesus said, "No one can serve two masters; for a slave will either hate the one and love the other, or be devoted to the one and despise the other. You cannot serve God and wealth" (Matthew 6:24). Everything and everyone exists for God and is in his care. When will we learn to live this fact and cease to be slaves to the anxieties of the world? However, because in Western society we think of false gods as weird looking statues, we must consider a few examples of false gods here. Self-importance and obsessive desires to be the best dressed, have the best home, car, job, stuff, retirement plan, etc., is the disordered pursuit of perfection, a false god. Our innate longing to achieve perfection is really our natural longing for God. This longing cannot be satisfied unless it is ordered toward God's perfection.

"You shall not bow down to them or worship them..." (Exodus 20:5). All sin is bowing down to false gods. "So God created humankind in his

image..." (Genesis 1:27). Since we alone are created in God's own image, what created thing can we bow down to without grievously insulting God??

God made everything! He made the sciences and made us curious so that we may discover him in the magnificence of creation, but do we appreciate God for his gifts? Or do we instead congratulate ourselves for developing antibiotics, vaccines, finding stem cells, and the minute particles that make up the universe. We did not *create* these things. We *discovered* the gifts God created. We make ourselves gods by our lack of gratitude! And let's not forget people who use scientific discovery to dismiss our Creator as non-existent. The only wisdom they accept is the wisdom of this world, but it is clearly known by simple observation that the things of this world turn to dust. Imagine looking into the dust for answers! What foolishness! Pray for the healing of their blindness.

Why do we embrace superstition? Fear of the number thirteen (triskaidekaphobia) is so common that some buildings skip the thirteenth floor. It is inane to reject the freedom God offers us to become slaves to irrational beliefs!

Idolatry includes fortune-telling, séances, Tarot cards, horoscopes, Ouija boards, palm reading and the occult. People seek to be God when they try to know the future. Such practices provide an opportunity for Satan to influence them; he loves it when people turn to him for favors. No creature knows the future! That knowledge is reserved for God who told the Israelites: "When you come into the land that the Lord your God is giving you, you must not learn to imitate the abhorrent practices of those nations. No one shall be found among you who makes a son or daughter pass through fire, or who practices divination, or is a soothsayer, or an augur, or a sorcerer, or one who casts spells, or who consults ghosts or spirits, or who seeks oracles from the dead. For whoever does these things is abhorrent to the Lord; it is because of such abhorrent practices that the Lord your God is driving them out before you" (Deuteronomy 18:9-12).

Before literacy was commonplace, crucifixes, paintings, and other holy images were used to teach Holy Scripture but we must always be mindful that paintings and statues are only a poor shadow of the glory they are trying to depict.

"... for I the Lord your God am a jealous God, punishing children for the iniquity of parents, to the third and the fourth generation of those who reject me, but showing steadfast love to the thousandth generation of those who love me and keep my commandments" (Exodus 20:5-6). Here God speaks of justice and mercy. Parents who reject God show their children an evil example and they will all suffer the consequences, but God will not allow that family to be lost forever. He will heal them. Their rebellion and the consequences are limited.

"You shall not make wrongful use of the name of the Lord your God, for the Lord will not acquit anyone who misuses his name" (Exodus 20:7). Read, understand, and take to heart this commandment. When we speak the name of our Trinitarian God, our Father's name, and the name of Jesus, and of the Holy Spirit, we must *not* speak carelessly. We must say God's name with the sincere reverence due to our Creator, our Redeemer, and our Sanctifier. Abuse of God's name demonstrates arrogant disrespect toward God as well as all humankind, made in God's own image. When people carelessly swear, curse, and use Jesus' name wrongly, they are speaking the language of Satan, which should never be uttered.

"Remember the sabbath day, and keep it holy. Six days you shall labor and do all your work. But the seventh day is a sabbath to the Lord your God; you shall not do any work—you, your son or your daughter, your male or female slave, your livestock, or the alien resident in your

towns. For in six days the Lord made heaven and earth, the sea, and all that is in them, but rested the seventh day; therefore the Lord blessed the sabbath day and consecrated it" (Exodus 20:8-11). Our Creator knows that we have trouble prioritizing. We get so wrapped up in busyness that we forget to take care of our family, our neighbors, even ourselves, and we forget him. God legislated a day off!

God commands us to keep Sunday holy for our physical and spiritual well-being, not to cause us difficulty, but to help us keep the things of this world in perspective, and to encourage our spiritual journey toward everlasting life.

God required that the Israelites rest on the seventh day of the week. The seventh day was their day to worship God. But the Old Covenant was fulfilled and the New Covenant established when Jesus shed his blood and rose from the dead. He made all things new by his Resurrection on Easter Sunday, and the formal launch of his Church on Pentecost Sunday. Thus, he sanctified the first day of the week.[35] To those who insist that the sabbath must be celebrated on Saturday, let them be reminded of what Jesus told the Pharisees, who were enraged that his disciples broke off heads of grain in the field on the sabbath because they were hungry: "Then he said to them, 'The sabbath was made for humankind, and not humankind for the sabbath; so the Son of Man is lord even of the sabbath" (Mark 2:27-28). So, if Jesus Christ chose to rise up from the dead on a Sunday, and chose a Sunday to send the Holy Spirit at the beginning of his Church, then so be it! Christians have a Sunday sabbath. Amen! What did Jesus do on the sabbath? He went to the Temple, worshipped our Father, read Scripture, and taught and healed his fellow Israelites. He angered the Pharisees by his acts of charity.[36] Evidently, some Pharisees felt that Mosaic Law forbade miraculous cures on the sabbath.[37] They imposed man-made rules rather than encouraging charity, and they neglected the spirit of God's commandments. Every Sunday is an opportunity to renew and build our relationship with God and develop charity in our human relationships.

How to Love Your Neighbor

"Honor your father and your mother, so that your days may be long in the land that the Lord your God is giving you" (Exodus 20:12). Note the placement of this commandment in the Decalogue. The previous commandments make our duty toward God clear. Beginning with this commandment, we are instructed in our duty toward our families and neighbors. Its placement, as first among the "how to love our neighbor" commandments, reminds us of the importance of family in God's plan of salvation.

God designed the family structure. He made Adam from the clay of the earth and gave him power over all of the animals, but Adam was still alone.[38] Eve was created from the body of Adam, from man's own flesh to complete him; and man completes woman according to God's natural order: "…and they become one flesh" (Genesis 2:24). Man and woman united in marriage are fruitful partners in their care for each other. "God blessed them, and God said to them, 'Be fruitful and multiply, and fill the earth and subdue it; …'" (Genesis 1:28). Together they cooperate in God's creative action and have children. This is the natural order.

With God's help, parents provide for their children's education, material welfare, and especially, for their spiritual journey. Sadly, modern cultural influences make Christian parenting a challenge. Parents have little control over what their children are taught in schools where the Great Corruption is accepted as the norm, especially the deception that all beliefs are truth. Children become confused. Another problem is popular entertainment that mocks the natural order. So-called children's programming portrays parents as incompetent, older adults as troublesome, and children as smarter than adults. Animals are portrayed as having human-like intelligence and emotions. Lawful authority is mocked, values are distorted, and violence is glorified. Program providers insist that parents are responsible for screening what their children see, but parents are overwhelmed by the sheer bombardment of nastiness! Solution? Refuse to accept immoral influences and say "No!" by not buying objectionable products. Pray together as a family. Find support in like-minded Christians. Educate children to be Christian warriors so that they are armed against evil and can make good choices. Utilize Christian entertainment rating services. Remaining faithful to Christ is not getting easier. Teach children to stand their ground. Teach them that God loves them and is worth their time and attention.

Honor God our Father. He invented parenting. A loving family is the reflection of God's love for his children. Children, honor your parents; respect those entrusted with your care, and be obedient, like Jesus was obedient to Mary and Joseph.[39] As you grow into adulthood, treat your parents with honor and you will be honoring yourselves. Parents, allow your children to blossom into mature Christians. It can be a painful road but love, trust in God, and prayer ease the way. Children, help your parents with love and patience.[40] "Children, obey your parents in the Lord, for this is right. 'Honor your father and mother'–this is the first commandment with a promise: 'so that it may be well with you and you may live long on the earth'" (Ephesians 6:1-3).

"You shall not murder" (Exodus 20:13). Of all the sins committed by humankind, murder is the most heinous. When we a take a human life, we make ourselves gods. Humankind is the epitome of creation made in the image and likeness of God, and God dwells within every soul. Why does that knowledge not prevent people from covering up his light with the filth

of sin? All sin would cease if people believed in the sanctity of God's presence within them!

For the sake of clarity, we had better establish a definition of murder. The sin of murder does not include the selfless acts of courage performed by those entrusted with our safety—law enforcement and the military. Their job is not to intentionally kill, but to protect the innocent, and the consequence can be the killing of aggressors. Murder is intentional killing. Reasonable self-protection that results in the death of an aggressor is not murder if the intent is limited to self-protection and the safety of others. Deaths that result from the protection of peoples who are in danger, including those in danger of mass starvation or potential victims of genocide, are not murder. Indeed, failing to act against such horrors can result in moral complicity. Imagine what the world would look like today if self-sacrificing soldiers had not risked their lives to confront the evils of the Third Reich and, more recently, the evils of terrorism. All those who offer their lives to save others are imitating Christ, who offered his life to save all humankind.

These are some of the sins of murder: Assault or killing for personal gain, convenience, vengeance, or reason other than justifiable self-defense or protection of the helpless is murder. Revenge and plotting revenge are sins of murder, no matter how they are depicted in popular entertainment. Careless and dangerous actions that can result in injury or death, like impaired driving or careless risk taking, as well as, enticing someone to engage in dangerous actions are sins of murder. Suicide violates God's law; however, the victim's mental state must be taken into account. Do not make judgments about people who commit suicide. Only God knows.

Deliberate abortion of an unborn child is murder. "Now the word of the Lord came to me saying, 'Before I formed you in the womb I knew you, and before you were born I consecrated you; I appointed you a prophet to the nations" (Jeremiah 1:4-5). God has a plan for each child, no matter how conceived or how inconvenient the timing seems. The deliberate abortion of a child is so unnatural that it places a terrible burden of guilt on the consciences of the individuals responsible. Without repentance, which is difficult because the people involved have to admit that they murdered a human child, the consequence is the loss of eternal life, the death of their souls. The modern day murders of unborn human children at the altar of convenience are no less horrifying to God than the pagan ritual sacrifices of children[41] that he condemns in scripture. Participating in or paying for an abortion, supporting or donating to pro-choice ideologies or political candidates, and even complacency contributes to the organized murder of human beings. And now, providers of abortion pills want to make abortion appear no worse than getting rid of a headache. Very convenient. Murder made easy!

In vitro fertilization (IVF), a process that produces more embryos than can be implanted in their mother, is murder. Human embryonic stem cell lines used in research come from four- or five-day-old embryos that are left over after IVF. The embryos' parents must decide what to do with the unused embryos. They can pay to have a facility store them frozen to keep them alive, defrost the embryos, which kills them, donate them to some-one else, or donate the embryos for stem cell research (California Institute for Regenerative Medicine). Government sponsors of human embry-onic stem cell (hESC) research imply that destroying the embryos is not immoral since the embryos are not the product of abortion. The California Institute for Regenerative Medicine says on its website, "Don't forget that the embryos were donated from IVF clinics. They had been rejected for implantation and were going to be destroyed, or the couple had decided to stop storing the embryos for future use. The embryos used to create embry-onic stem cell lines *were already destined to be destroyed*"[42] (California Institute for Regenerative Medicine). Where is the human person consid-ered in this statement?

On August 9, 2001, U.S. President George W. Bush decreed that U.S. taxpayer money could be used for hESC research but limited that research to existing stem cell lines (National Institutes of Health). On June 20, 2007, President Bush issued Executive Order 13435 expanding hESC research but also specified some moral and ethical boundaries, stating in Section 2(d), "human embryos and fetuses, as living member of the human species, are not raw materials to be exploited or commodities to be bought and sold" (Bush). On March 9, 2009, President Barak Obama issued Executive Order 13505 revoking former President Bush's limitations. The National Institute of Health (NIH) was ordered to expand support for hESC research and to come up with its own ethical guidelines (Obama). What are NIH's ethical considerations regarding hESC research? The NIH website refers the reader to the policy developed by the National Academy of Sciences Guidelines for Human Embryonic Stem Cell Research, which seems very concerned with maintaining stem cell lines that meet Congressional hESC research funding guidelines (Raynard S. Kingston). Individual states that have funded hESC research, avoiding Congressional restrictions, include California, Connecticut, Illinois, Maryland, New Jersey, and New York (Health Day).

How did people come to accept the murder of these tiny human beings so casually? Firstly, IVF was touted as a popular "good" because it, like abortion, seemed to solve a problem. If a loving couple wants children, they should be allowed to do what is necessary to have children. But because IVF results in the destruction of human embryos, the conscience of the populace had to be numbed to the fact these embryos are human beings, so just like the abortion argument, the rhetoric calls human embryos a mass of formless cells to dehumanize them. In fact, just seventeen days after a human embryo is implanted in its mother, this mass of formless cells produces a beating human heart, that is, twenty-four days after the new person is conceived (New Health Guide). And, lest government or hESC researchers be found guilty of killing babies, accepted ethical guidelines require that the embryos' parents give un-coerced permission for the embryos they conceived to be killed (Raynard S. Kingston). Once the populace is convinced to close their eyes to the murder of human embryos, it is not much of a leap to decide that left over human embryos should be put to good use. The thought of using unwanted human embryos to cure disease eases the conscience of the populace. Private researchers loudly proclaim yet unproven medical cures that might be discovered by hESC research and receive huge grants.

Pressure from special interest lobbies opened the door to taxpayer funding of hESC research, which was limited to the existing stem cell lines in an absurd attempt to establish ethical guidelines in a decidedly unethical arena. Research permissions were soon expanded a little more, but there was still mention of a moral duty to the unborn human being. A few years later, the conscience of the populace had grown so self-justified that federal funding could once again be expanded, and restrictions on hESC research decreased so profoundly that it seems the government and the populace no longer recognize that the embryos being experimented upon are fully human!

Would researchers and government have us believe that God withholds souls from embryos whose parents choose to freeze for later use? IVF embryos are a woman's egg fertilized by a man's sperm, but in a lab rather than in the human body. The implanted embryos grow into fully human children, not soulless monsters! The discarded human embryo and its anointed purpose are defrosted and die, or it is killed so it can become part of medical experiments. Each human embryo has a specific DNA map, and in the tiny package of the fertilized egg exists the DNA code of a specifically talented human being. And what of parents who choose not to give their children a chance to be born? They console themselves by thinking that giving permission to use their discarded embryos for hESC research will help the sick. Who are they to say that their frozen unborn child would not have done greater things to help humankind?! Humankind is pretending it can manipulate God and his natural order! God made the rules! There are no soulless embryos! God always cooperates in the act of conception by providing a human soul without which an embryo could not live. DNA in the embryo is the formation map but a human soul is required for life.

For couples who desire children, being unable to conceive is painful beyond words. However, considering IVF is not the answer. The same generous love that brings about the desire to have children is horrified at the thought of murdering them. IVF is a very selfish act, not an act of love. It is the ruthless act of doing whatever is necessary to achieve the parents' desires, without counting the cost. Perhaps the childless couple is being called to adopt or foster children. Do not risk your souls! Trust in God and desire his Will for you. God will lead you to fulfillment if you are patient enough to allow him.

Promoters of the Great Corruption would have us accept the evil notion that the desires of parents override the interests of the unborn. Government imposes this inhuman ideology upon taxpayers to justify spending taxpayer dollars to fund perverse ideological causes like abortion and human embryonic stem cell research. Advances in adult stem cell research have produced actual cures! People are now being cured of severe spinal injuries and other serious conditions using their own stem cells. Why pursue hESC research then? So that medical supply and drug companies can mass-produce generic lines of stem cell cures, a real boon for corporate profits!

Frozen embryos and unborn children are treated like slaves, as property to dispose of as their owners, a.k.a. biological parents, desire! In 1857, slave Dred Scott petitioned the Supreme Court of the United States for his freedom because he had lived in a free state with his owner before they returned to a slave state. He argued that having lived in a free state entitled him to emancipation. The decision of the court was shocking. The Court ruled 7-2 that no black person, slave or free, was a U.S. citizen therefore no black person, slave or free, had the right to petition the Court, nor were they owed any of the other protections and rights accorded to citizens of the United States (Dred Scott Case). Slavery, though intrinsically evil, was legal and acceptable to the populace at that time because it was a convenient and lucrative way to solve the problem of needed cheap farm labor. Abolitionists, enraged at the Supreme Court's Dred Scott decision, opposed the slavery industry. Their efforts awakened moral outrage against the cruelty of slavery, but it took a violent civil war to free the enslaved people. The violence done to society by the evil of slavery is still not undone many generations later. In 1973, the Supreme Court decision, Roe vs. Wade, took away the rights and protections of citizenship from unborn members of our society. The abortion industry now provides a convenient and lucrative way to provide the final solution to unwanted children, but advances in medical technology and DNA research clearly reveal that the human embryo, even at the earliest stages of development, is a fully human being. What will it take to awaken public moral outrage against the cruelty of voluntary abortions and stop the intrinsically evil murder of our children? How long will it take for society to recover from the loss of so much talent and potential?

Two young co-workers were at lunch. Sally saw that her friend Beth seemed preoccupied and asked her, "What's the matter?"

"I'm pregnant," sighed Beth.

"Really? Are you going to keep it?" Sally asked.[43]

Not long ago, the announcement of a pregnancy would have led to congratulations and questions like, "Do you want a boy or a girl?" How horrifying it is that abortion is now so casual an option!

Wake up, Christians! Voluntary abortion is not about rape, or incest, or protecting the life of the mother as the corruptors claim. It is about whether the child's father takes responsibility for his actions and cares for his child or is so self-centered that he tries to wriggle out of his parental responsibility because fatherhood does not fit conveniently into his plans. It is about whether the child's mother is generous enough to accept the gift of an unexpected child by adjusting her plans. It is about whether they are human enough to take responsibility for the consequences of their decisions! Believing that abortion on demand is a human kindness to women is the ultimate corrupted thinking. Human kindness demands practical assistance and physical and emotional support for all parents and their unborn children, not murderous options.

Corruptors of the truth would have you believe that the life of an unborn child is without value. Many who long for children and suffer the pain of childlessness would argue that children so ardently desired cannot be without value. To explain simply: Mr. and Mrs. X want a swimming pool. They work hard to save money and finally have enough, but when they apply for a permit, the county tells them that they do not have enough property to build a pool. The X's are disappointed, but their neighbors, Mr. and Mrs. Y, have an abundance of property. They own a swimming pool but have decided to fill it with dirt and plant grass over it because it is too troublesome to maintain. The X's are willing to lease the land with the pool. With cooperation from their neighbors, the X's could have a pool and the Y's would have additional cash flow without responsibility for the upkeep of the pool. The Y's decide to fill in their pool anyway. They realize that they have reduced the value of their property and that they have lost the chance for additional cash flow. They also know Mr. and Mrs. X are disappointed at losing their chance of having a pool.

In this example, the pool represents a child. Mr. and Mrs. X are all those who desire children. Mr. and Mrs. Y represent people considering abortion. People, not only mothers, because aborted human beings have fathers, relatives, medical providers, and others who are responsible for their deaths. Filling the pool with dirt is aborting the child. The reduced property value is the physical, emotional, and spiritual trauma caused by destroying a child. No matter how casually abortion providers treat the matter, abortion has serious physical, emotional, and spiritual consequences. Unless the mother is a sociopath, a bond is formed with the new life in her body. There are physical and psychological changes that make her aware of the presence of a new life. She can try to fool herself into thinking it is not a human being, but her conscience makes her know that she is carrying a fully human child. The loss of cash flow is the loss of God's grace, that is, the destruction of the plan God had for this child and the good he/she would have offered humankind. Those who cooperate in the abortion also reject God's grace and make their souls unreceptive to other graces God wants to send them. Without repentance, which as explained above, is difficult, the murderers' souls are lost.

Wake up, Christians! The demonstrators' signs at a pro-choice rally read, "My child, my choice." Pro-choice is not about making a choice. This perverted thinking must stop! The demonstrators' signs clearly acknowledge that they want the "choice" to murder unborn children with impunity! Pro-choice is murder sanctioned by the populace! The only true choice is whether the parents will raise their child or allow adoption. Financial problems? Many loving people are willing to help women make arrangements to receive medical care and physical and emotional support while they are pregnant. Seek out a pro-life pregnancy center. No child is a mistake! God does not abandon the woman who has the courage to bear an unplanned child. He doubly blesses her for her generous love.

Euthanasia is murder. In one court, a judge denies permission to withdraw hydration and nutrition from a woman in a minimally conscious state, while in another a judge orders that hydration and nutrition be withheld from a woman in a similar condition.[44] Walking away from God's commandments has caused injustice and confusion. Confusion does not come from God; it is Satan's tool! Euthanasia, assisted suicide, and neglect of the helpless are all sins of murder. What human being has the right to decide when a human life is no longer worthwhile? If we push God's Will aside and embrace government-supported euthanasia, judges will decide whose life is worth living. Government-supported euthanasia requires an objective metric to determine whose lives are worthwhile. Who determines the metric? The same judges who legalized abortion? Government-supported euthanasia is not a far-fetched idea. It is already legal is some places. In 1965, the populace believed that abortion was evil, never imagining that, within a decade, abortion on demand would be made a "right" by the U.S. Supreme Court. Even now, health insurance industry employees decide which patients receive needed medications prescribed by their physicians and which patients do not. A society's strength is measured by its compassion. We make ourselves weak!

Murder is the result of choosing anger, hatred, jealousy, self-centeredness, greed, vengefulness, and a violent lifestyle. These sins are symptomatic of a people who have abandoned God. Human authority and laws cannot stop violence; governments are powerless to make laws that can dictate and enforce a loving, peaceful spirit, selflessness, compassion, and kindliness upon the populace! Stopping the violence calls for an enthusiastic grass roots spiritual movement. It calls for Christian action! It calls for obedience to God's commandments!

This is how Jesus interprets the commandment against murder for us: "You have heard that it was said to those of ancient times, 'You shall not murder'; and 'whoever murders shall be liable to judgment.' But I say to you that if you are angry with a brother or sister, you will be liable to judgment; and if you insult a brother or sister, you will be liable to the council; and if you say, 'You fool,' you will be liable to the hell of fire" (Matthew 5:21-22).

God expects us to get along with one another, to love one another. We must love our enemies out of respect for God and his creative goodness; love the individuals but despise their sinful actions. It may not be advisable to associate with one's enemies; we must oppose evil and avoid its influence and dangers, but we must not hate our enemies, plot against them, or wish them ill. Pray that they will open their hearts to the light of Christ.

"You shall not commit adultery." Jesus said, "You have heard that it was said, 'You shall not commit adultery.' But I say to you that everyone who looks at a woman with lust has already committed adultery with her in his heart" (Matthew 5:27-28).

In modern society, "having sex" means participating in the sexual act. The words are casually spoken without regard for the deeply spiritual commitment involved. God designed the creative act to form the building blocks of family. When a man and woman are united and become one body in the sexual act, the union is much more than physical. God designed the sexual act to change who they are and help them unlock their hearts and souls, to become open and vulnerable to one another, emotionally, spiritually, and physically, so the two can become one. God designed this sharing to be enjoyable and fulfilling. It is a great perversion to regard such an intimate sharing as casual entertainment.

"Do you not know that your bodies are members of Christ? Should I therefore take the members of Christ and make them members of a prostitute? Never! Do you not know that whoever is united to a prostitute becomes one body with her? For it is said, 'The two shall be one flesh.' But anyone united to the Lord becomes one spirit with him. Shun fornication! Every sin that a person commits is outside the body; but the fornicator sins against the body itself. Or do you not know that your body is a temple of the Holy Spirit within you, which you have from God, and that you are not your own? For you were bought with a price; therefore, glorify God in your body" (1 Corinthians 6:15-20). The price was the crucifixion of Jesus.

Adultery and fornication are not about pure, genuine love no matter how romantic popular culture makes them seem. They are about the selfishness and self-deception that wound genuine love. Any voluntary sexual act outside of the marriage covenant is a rejection of God's eternal design and is sinful. However, if the act does occur, and the woman becomes pregnant, abortion is not the solution! That would only place the offenders' souls in greater jeopardy. Two wrongs do not make a right. The offenders should seek forgiveness and the welfare of the child. We cannot understand God's plan. Look at the ancestors of Jesus. Some were very imperfect, but they gave us our Savior.

The marriage covenant must be undertaken with full acceptance and understanding of the responsibilities and the commitment being made to spouse, to family, and to God. Careless marriages offend God. The Lord said to the people of Israel around the fifth century B.C.: "And this you do as well: You cover the Lord's altar with tears, with weeping and groaning because he no longer regards the offering or accepts it with favor at your hand. You ask, 'Why does he not?' Because the Lord was a witness between you and the wife of your youth, to whom you have been faithless, though she is your companion and your wife by covenant. Did not one God make her? Both flesh and spirit are his. And what does the one God desire? Godly offspring. So look to yourselves, and do not let anyone be faithless to the wife of his youth. For I hate divorce, says the Lord, the God of Israel, and covering one's garment with violence, says the Lord of hosts. So take heed to yourselves and do not be faithless" (Malachi 2:13-16).

Jesus restated God's original design: "Some Pharisees came, and to test him they asked, 'Is it lawful for a man to divorce his wife?' He answered them, 'What did Moses command you?' They said, 'Moses allowed a man to write a certificate of dismissal and to divorce her.' But Jesus said to them, 'Because of your hardness of heart he wrote this commandment for you. But from the beginning of creation, 'God made them male and female.'

'For this reason a man shall leave his father and mother and be joined to his wife, and the two shall become one flesh.' So they are no longer two, but one flesh. Therefore what God has joined together, let no one separate.' Then in the house the disciples asked him again about this matter. He said to them, 'Whoever divorces his wife and marries another commits adultery against her; and if she divorces her husband and marries another, she commits adultery'" (Mark 10:2-12).

Divorce damages society. Long term studies of the children of divorce conclude that they suffer from "fears of betrayal, abandonment, loss, and rejection," "rising anxiety in late teens and early 20s–feelings and memories about their parents' divorce arise with new intensity as they enter adulthood," "lifelong vulnerability to the experience of loss," "anger, resentment, and hostility," "a reduction in psychological well-being," "depression in young adulthood," "low life satisfaction," as well as "fear of commitment and intimacy," "less trust in future spouse," and "reduction in inhibitions toward divorce as a solution for marital difficulties" (Matthews). Divorce begets divorces. Observing their parents' love teaches children about God's love, and teaches them to trust. Divorce teaches that love is conditional and trust is absurd. High divorce rates are a recipe for societal failure.

Jesus commands us to love one another and no exception is made for an irritating spouse. A baptized man and woman united in the marriage covenant enjoy a unique gift that draws them together in love. God never takes back the gift of marital love; divorce rejects it. Divorce makes a mockery of the trust God places in the married couple. Sadly, betrayals occur. When a spouse endangers or abandons his/her family, civil divorce might be necessary to gain physical and legal protections for the innocent spouse and children. However, civil divorce does not terminate the spiritual marriage covenant. It is possible that one or both spouses made insincere vows or lacked the maturity to understand the seriousness of the marital commitment or made vows with careless or evil intent. In such cases, it is possible that there is no true marital covenant. Consult a pastor for guidance.

The term "gay marriage" is a mockery of God's gift of marriage. There is no creative purpose. There is no unselfish generative purpose. God does not bless gay marriages because they are contrary to his natural Law, even if they are performed in a church. God is not a hypocrite, but people can be. In Scripture, same-sex sexual relationships are condemned in strong terms. Here are a few direct passages:

Leviticus 18:22: "You shall not lie with a male as with a woman; it is an abomination."

Romans 1:27: "Men committed shameless acts with men and received in their own persons the due penalty for their error."

1 Timothy 1:8-11: "Now we know that the law is good, if one uses it legitimately. This means understanding that the law is laid down not for the innocent but for the lawless and disobedient, for the godless and sinful, for the unholy and profane, for those who kill their mother or father, for murderers, fornicators, sodomites, slave traders, liars, perjurers, and whatever else is contrary to the sound teaching that conforms to the glorious Gospel of the blessed God, which he entrusted to me."

It is ridiculous to believe that Jesus accepts or condones same-sex sexual relationships. God's Law forbids it! Jesus did not come to change God's Law but to fulfill it. When Jesus forgave the woman who was about to be stoned for committing adultery, he was not condoning adultery. He told her not to commit adultery again.[45] "Having sex" outside of marriage is sinful! God loves us and forgives us, but that does not give people carte blanche to violate his Law. God forgives those who repent and make a sincere effort to change their sinful ways. Those who defy God's commandments reject forgiveness and choose the works of Satan.

Simply being homosexual is not a sin, but a fact for some. These individuals are called to chastity like any other unmarried individual. Sexual relationship is not a civil right but a spiritual gift within the state of holy marriage. Any other attitude toward the sexual act endangers eternal salvation. There is no authentic love outside of God's commandments, only inhuman lust.

"Do you not know that wrongdoers will not inherit the kingdom of God? Do not be deceived! Fornicators, idolaters, adulterers, male prostitutes, sodomites, thieves, the greedy, drunkards, revilers, robbers–none of these will inherit the kingdom of God" (1 Corinthians 6:9-10). These perversions that earn hell for souls are so popular nowadays that they propel books to top-seller status and generate big box office profits for movies! How out of touch humankind is with God's design! How many times a day are adults and children bombarded by media images designed to invite sinful thoughts and actions? Human trafficking, prostitution, pornography, rape, and sexual abuse are the consequences of acceptance by the populace of a greatly perverted view of human sexuality. Sexual perversion will not stop until the populace rejects all ungodly sexual representations and accepts the Truth that humankind is created in the image and likeness of God and the human sexual act is deserving of respectful dignity! No deceitful justification or manipulation can change God's Truth or make evil acceptable in the eyes of God! There are grave issues here. Jesus said, "If any of you put a stumbling block before one of these little ones who believe in me, it would be better for you if a great millstone were fastened around your neck and you were drowned in the depth of the sea. Woe to the world because of stumbling blocks! Occasions for stumbling are bound to come, but woe to the one by whom the stumbling block comes!" (Matthew 18:6-7). The time is now to consider whether you are a stumbling block. Ask yourself, "Do I actively or passively participate in or tolerate evil?" The time to repent is now, and the time to take corrective action is now! Don't wait for the "Woe!"

The previous two commandments defend humankind's most essential principles–the dignity of human life without which humanity is animalistic, and the dignity of the human family without which social justice is non-existent. But the commandments govern much more than interpersonal dealings. They prescribe the appropriate code of conduct and moral responsibility for societies, governments, financial institutions, businesses and corporations, workers and business owners, political and religious institutions, the wealthy and the poor. In other words, every human being and every human contrivance must be governed by the Ten Commandments.

"You shall not steal. You shall not bear false witness against your neighbor" (Exodus 20:15-16). Reputation is the character of an individual as perceived by his/her community. A good reputation means that the individual person is respected, and so has the opportunity to interact with community members, earn a living, and be successful. However, reputations are easily damaged by people who misjudge, are jealous, overly sensitive, vengeful, or uncharitable. Careless words can harm the reputation of an innocent person and cause suffering. "For every species of bird and beast, of reptile and sea creature, can be tamed and has been tamed by the human species, but no one can tame the tongue—a restless evil, full of deadly poison. With it we bless the Lord and Father, and with it we curse those who are made in the likeness of God" (James 3:7-10). Evil words come from an evil heart[46] and gossip is evil, no matter how popular it has become. Gossip is stealing a person's reputation. Whether one gossips about celebrities in the media or individuals at the water cooler, it is a perversion against God's commandments. Jesus said, "I tell you, on the day of judgment you will have to give an account for every careless word you utter; for by your words you will be justified, and by your words you will

be condemned" (Matthew 12:36-37). Be generous when you speak about other people, for your own sake!

Boundaries are part of societal order. Children naturally believe that everything was created for their amusement and must be taught limits. They are taught not to take property that does not belong to them and that they do not have a right to tell lies. The lessons are hard learned because young children lie and steal to get what makes them feel good, and everyone wants to feel good. Maturity brings the realization that not everything that feels good is good.

Young children do not understand the societal consequences of lying and stealing. They do understand that lying and stealing gets them what they want right now, and they realize that the consequences of their minor crimes cause them pain. For example: the new family on the block has three children, all under age ten, who walk into their neighbors' homes and take food or toys without permission. The shocked neighbors must now lock their doors to keep their property safe. The children have food and toys of their own but believe that if they like something they are entitled to it. Their neglectful parents have not taught them respect for others. The individual consequence? The neighbors resent the children's bad behavior and the children suffer rejection. The societal consequence? The neighborhood loses its peace.

It falls to the family, the basis of all society, to teach children honesty, integrity, generosity, compassion, respect for themselves and others, and self-control, i.e., virtues. This requires formation of children's consciences by responsible adults who live God's commandments. These virtues must be instilled in children to develop their personal integrity, which, in general, maintains societal order. Without common virtues, societal boundaries become vague and are easily circumvented resulting in confusion, corruption, and anarchy. This is happening today in our schools, in our centers of philosophy and higher learning, in our halls of justice, in our political and governmental apparatus, and last but not least, in our families, the building blocks of our society, that are under ruthless and painful attack. Virtue and integrity are being violently redefined by the Great Corruption.

Individuals who stand up for Truth are slandered; they are discredited, and labeled with hideous descriptions with no meaningful or factual basis. The most obvious example is the false claim of racial division put forth by LGBT rights promoters. LGBT rights advocates claim that Christians are hate-mongers, who would deprive them of their civil rights. They defy commandments and laws that have been on the books for thousands of years, deny their legitimacy, and pervert them in the name of social justice to serve their own agenda while, at the same time, denying Christians their religious civil rights. Hypocrisy! LGBT promoters compare their effort to change social values with the great Civil Rights movement in the United States. The problem with that thinking is that enslaving people is sinful. Abolition and the Civil Rights movements were legitimate demands to restore human rights and reputation to an entire segment of the population and correct a societal failure of morality. The LGBT movement demands that society accept a newly invented morality and set of behaviors that have been rejected as sinful for thousands of years. There is no moral basis for the imposition of their demands. They are, in fact, demanding that their sinful practices be accepted by society as a normal way of behavior. Corruptors, who reject the common virtues and God's commandments, have no legitimate basis upon which to function in society. They are like the children who lie and steal because it makes them feel good. They do not consider weighing their lustful desires against the damage they are doing to their victims or societal order. Their perception of good and evil changes on a whim. This chaos afflicts our society now. God is all virtue. Without God, there is no virtue and, in recent years, God has been rejected or has been relegated to a position in the closet to be pulled out in times of disaster when people think he is needed. The result is an infection of injustice in society.

Christians are God's community. When Christians unite and acknowledge their complete dependence upon God and obey his commandments, they will be a force to reckon with as a unified Christian people oppose the perpetrators and perversions of the Great Corruption. The time for Christians to unite in God's Truth and oppose evil is now! Corruptors have already made laws that outlaw Christian morality and have made criminals of Christians. Christians have the God-given right to practice their faith in every aspect of their daily lives without molestation, and to raise their children to know, love, and serve God in this life as heirs to the eternal happiness Christ promised without being harassed and persecuted by ungodly people and governments. They have the right to their legal property, to earn an honest living at a fair rate of pay without prejudice, to engage in honest trade without being subjected to immoral civil laws that violate the Christian conscience and threaten their assets and livelihood. They have the right to enjoy a secure place to live, work, and worship God without being violently attacked, and to enjoy the gifts God gives in this life. Only universal obedience to God's commandments secures these rights for all.

The Great Corruption is already well entrenched in our society. The populace is becoming so accustomed to living with calumny and theft that they do not even recognize the perverse circumstances around them. For example:

Self-serving leaders and politicians accrue great wealth because they have the power to offer favors to people who donate. They set up their legal entities and foundations, but they neglect their responsibility to work for the greater good of their constituents because they prefer their own good. Some even believe that their own good is what's best for all. These self-serving politicians are stealing from their constituents, who place their welfare and futures in their leaders' hands.

Financial institutions have "factored out" the welfare of humanity. Families, forced to pay outrageous interest rates on the purchase of a home, tripling the original price of the home over the term of the loan, are having their freedom, quality of life, and economic futures stolen by financial institutions in what amounts to an economic holocaust. This is institutional thievery.

Credit scoring is a capricious evaluator of a person's reliability. Consolidating the mind, heart and soul of a person into a three-digit number is intrinsically evil. (Think 666). A poor score can keep a person from getting a job, vehicle insurance, make it impossible to buy or rent a home, and steals away a productive future. In addition, the victims of credit fraud or a poor credit score must fight unresponsive institutions to correct careless errors that profoundly affect their lives. Credit scoring is the worst kind of calumny and amounts to institutional thievery.

Advertising that misleads and promotes the selling of products, that fail to perform as promised, is institutional thievery. The common warning is "Let the buyer beware!" Does that mean that we are to accept the intrinsic evil of deceptive advertising? What a sad commentary on the practices of commercial enterprise and the willingness of human beings to lie and accept liars!

Many governmental and commercial entities require that individuals provide personal information in order to obtain jobs or receive necessary products or services, including medical care. Entities that fail to adequately protect their clients' personal information, by their carelessness, are complicit in the theft of their clients' identities. This is institutional thievery by neglect.

Federal and local governments impose complicated and intrusive tax codes that are constantly changed in order to manipulate taxpayers and the economy. They place heavy burdens upon anxious taxpayers who can never be sure what the rules are. If they miscalculate, taxpayers are subjected to expensive fines and penalties. In addition, taxing organizations have outrageous leeway to manipulate the intent of the tax law by reinterpreting it when they write regulations. Favored taxpayers[47] get away with owing millions of dollars without significant consequences, while middle class taxpayers lose their small paychecks and their homes to government levies or property tax liens because they owe a few thousand dollars.

Workplaces are rife with theft and calumny. Thieving workers take long breaks, neglect their work, and expect their co-workers to pick up the slack. They are stealing from their employers and co-workers, who must do their own jobs as well as the work assigned to the thieves. Resentment ensues and the peace of the workplace is lost. Thieving employers demand that their employees complete their assignments by unreasonable deadlines and refuse to pay for overtime. To keep their jobs, their employees work many unpaid hours. The employer is guilty of the theft of the employees' talents, of the time they should be spending with their families, and of their future well-being. Abusing the time and trust of one's neighbor in the workplace is thievery. Honest business relationships are the sign of a healthy society that honors virtue and integrity.

Pete and Jack purchased a business. For a time, they did well as partners, until Pete decided he wanted more and began to steal some of their business income. Afraid that Jack would figure it out and report his thefts to the police, Pete suddenly took all of the money out of their joint business bank account and deposited into an account he opened in only his name. He contacted their bank, suppliers, customers, and the police and aggressively accused Jack of the crimes that Pete had himself committed, but, of course, did not file criminal action against Jack. He changed the alarm system and locked Jack out of their office. Jack hired an attorney, but Pete had physical possession of the business and the business' money and assets. Jack struggled to defend himself against false accusations. The business' customers and suppliers no longer trusted Jack because of Pete's calumny. Overnight Jack lost his investment in the business and his job. After several years of paying lawyers, Jack could no longer afford to fight in civil courts. Pete succeeded in stealing the business with the aid of attorneys and judges who accepted Pete, the liar with the money, over Jack, the righteous man, who fought for the just return of his property within an unjust legal system. This is a true story. The names are changed. This is calumny committed by Pete and everyone who repeated his lies, deception, and thievery abetted by a civil court system where the person with the most money wins.

These are just a few examples of the imaginative ways human beings have developed to destroy each other. Institutional sin is pervasive. Dishonesty and calumny is pandemic, infecting every corner of the world, stealing the peace, security, and freedom God meant for humankind to enjoy. Every human person and institution has an obligation to be guided by God's commandments! "Have we not all one Father? Has not one God created us? Why then are we faithless to one another, profaning the covenant of our ancestors?" (Malachi 2:10). Humankind knows God's Truth—it is written in our hearts—yet develops innumerable ways to sin against it.

Christians are commissioned at baptism to be prophets, and prophets teach by words and example. Be a good prophet. Do not compromise! "Beware of false prophets, who come to you in sheep's clothing but inwardly are ravenous wolves. You will know them by their fruits. Are grapes gathered from thorns, or figs from thistles? In the same way, every good tree bears good fruit, but the bad tree bears bad fruit. A good tree cannot bear bad fruit, nor can a bad tree bear good fruit. Every tree that does not bear good fruit is cut down and thrown into the fire. Thus you will know them by their fruits" (Matthew 7:15-21). The "bad fruit?" "Now the works of the flesh are obvious: fornication, impurity, licentiousness, idolatry, sorcery, enmities, strife, jealousy, anger, quarrels, dissensions, factions, envy, drunkenness, carousing, and things like these. I am warning you, as I warned you before: those who do such things will not inherit the kingdom of God" (Galatians 5:19-21). The "good fruit?" "By contrast, the fruit of the Spirit is love, joy, peace, patience, kindness, generosity, faithfulness, gentleness, and self-control..." (Galatians 5:22-23). Those who claim to be Christian and do not obey the commandments are "bad fruit" people. They are liars who bear false witness against Christ, against our Father in heaven, and against the Holy Spirit. "Good fruit" people obey God's word and give effective witness to God's Truth.[48]

What can be done? Remember the advice Jesus gave his disciples when he sent them out to proclaim the Good News, "See, I am sending you out like sheep into the midst of wolves; so be wise as serpents and innocent as doves" (Matthew 10:16). Strive to correct error, keep your heart pure, and patiently endure what you cannot change. Count on God's help! Courageously adhere to God's commandments and do not compromise with the perversions of the Great Corruption. The simple life is best. Be honest in your thoughts and dealings because Christ judges thoughts and deeds. Above all, pray for wisdom and discern the Will of God. Use your time and talents well. Do not pretend that you are what you are not. We cannot achieve holiness if we do not understand who and what we are. Be greedy for holy love because holy love is an eternal investment. "Do not love the world or the things in the world. The love of the Father is not in those who love the world; for all that is in the world–the desire of the flesh, the desire of the eyes, the pride in riches–comes not from the Father but from the world. And the world and its desire are passing away, but those who do the will of God live forever" (1 John 2:15-17).

If conflict should arise among Christians, remember what Jesus said: "If another member of the church sins against you, go and point out the fault when the two of you are alone. If the member listens to you, you have regained that one. But if you are not listened to, take one or two others along with you, so that every word may be confirmed by the evidence of two or three witnesses. If the member refuses to listen to them, tell it to the church; and if the offender refuses to listen even to the church, let such a one be to you as a Gentile and a tax collector" (Matthew 18:15-17). If the offenders absolutely refuse to listen, then they separate themselves from the Christian community. If fellow Christians are sinning, then we have an obligation to pray for them and, if possible, help them see their error, not as judges, but charitably, as Jesus commands.

Sadly, there is no pathway of correction to help those who do not believe in God's commandments. They reject the Truth and close the door on reason. As the populace moves away from Christ, they move away from the pathway to peace Christ offers. Without Christ, there can be no peace, only chaos.

"You shall not covet your neighbor's house; you shall not covet your neighbor's wife, or male or female slave, or ox, or donkey, or anything that belongs to your neighbor" (Exodus 20:17). Covet means to desire something excessively without regard for the rights of others. Remember the "bad fruit" people? The self-serving politicians, greedy financial institutions, calumniating credit reporting agencies, lying advertisers, neglectful governmental agencies and businesses, thieving employers and employees, and the corrupt governmental taxing agencies? They aggressively and greedily contrive plots against God's Law without regard for their victims' God-given rights. This institutional sin is accepted by the populace because of our cultural tolerance of deception and manipulation as normal. Not only that, governments and courts make and enforce evil laws that sanction institutional sin and the resulting evil deeds! Christians who refuse to bow down to greedy institutions suffer under their heavy-handed tactics. Up and coming generations do not stand a chance. Evil is written into laws and tax codes! Must we accept aggressive greed as a way of life? Covetousness has gone institutional and institutional sin is stealing our collective peace!

God-given rights are accorded to humankind by God's natural order and reflect the dignity of the human person. They are delineated by the Ten Commandments. Human laws that violate God's commandments diminish human rights and deny God-given human dignity.

Back to Pete: Pete sinned by coveting more than his share of the partnership's income. In our culture, financial success in business is honored, and Pete coveted wealth and success more than honesty and integrity. In his mind, success required that he take the business for himself. He justified his plans by thinking, "Jack doesn't work as hard as I do and doesn't deserve to be a full partner," and, "This business does not make enough profit to support two families and something has to be done." Having convinced himself that he was justified, he increased his sinfulness by stealing profits from his partner. When he became fearful that he might be caught, he did not repent. Instead, he concocted a complicated scheme to steal the business away from Jack entirely. The lawsuit went on for years and Pete sinned in every continuing act of theft and calumny he made against Jack. But Pete's downfall began with coveting more than his share. Sin darkened his heart until he no longer recognized sin. Jesus said, "For out of the heart come evil intentions, murder, adultery, fornication, theft, false witness, slander (Matthew 15:19). Many unfortunate people live with darkened hearts. Their arrogance and lack of repentance blinds them and destroys any ambition for heavenly things. And Jack? Through the grace of God, Jack was able to move his family to a new town and begin a new successful business. He lives peacefully retired now and trusts in God's justice.

Obeying the Ten Commandments removes spiritual blindness. Repentance and the heartfelt intention to obey God draw his grace and mercy. Never be discouraged by sinfulness. Remember, God reached out to us first. "For God so loved the world that he gave his only Son, so that everyone who believes in him may not perish but may have eternal life. Indeed, God did not send the Son into the world to condemn the world, but in order that the world might be saved through him" (John 3:16-17). Do not fear. Repent and embrace God's mercy. Trust in his love for you. Once we have tasted the freedom of belonging to Christ, all the world's treasures become useless junk to shed, as we are unburdened in mind and heart through God's grace, and draw closer to the Kingdom of God and gaining everything in Christ Jesus.[49] Amen!

CHAPTER 8

The Grace of Church

" Therefore thus says the Lord God, See, I am laying in Zion a foundation stone, a tested stone, a precious cornerstone, a sure foundation: 'One who trusts will not panic'" (Isaiah 28:16).

Jesus Established His Church

Any person who starts a new business takes care to protect the venture by establishing an organizational structure, and carefully choosing corporate officers and a board of directors through whom the future purpose and existence of the business can be guaranteed long after the original incorporator is gone. Why would Jesus do any less for his people? Jesus was born to teach, heal, suffer and die to redeem us, rise from the dead, and to establish the organizational structure that guarantees future generations will experience God's Truth as Jesus taught it.

Remember the children's game where a secret is whispered from one person to the next? By the time the whisper reaches the last person, the secret is usually distorted. People interpret what they hear differently and repeat their own interpretation. Jesus' Church safeguards God's Word by the power of the Holy Spirit so that God's Word is passed from one generation to the next without misinterpretation and error.

To form the Church, Jesus began by gathering disciples who accepted his invitation to "Follow me."[50] Many accepted the invitation and Jesus taught them by word and example to share the good news. Jesus then chose the members of the board: "And when day came, he called his disciples and chose twelve of them, whom he also named apostles: Simon, whom he named Peter, and his brother Andrew, and James, and John, and Philip, and Bartholomew, and Matthew, and Thomas, and James son of Alphaeus, and Simon, who was called the Zealot, and Judas son of James, and Judas Iscariot, who became a traitor" (Luke 6:13-16).

Next Jesus chose the head of the board of directors: "Now when Jesus came into the district of Caesarea Philippi, he asked his disciples, 'Who do people say that the Son of Man is?'" (Matthew 16:13). Their answers varied from John the Baptist to one of the ancient prophets but "Simon Peter answered, 'You are the Messiah, the Son of the living God.' And Jesus answered him, 'Blessed are you, Simon, son of Jonah! For flesh and blood has not revealed this to you, but my Father in heaven. And I tell you, you are Peter, and on this rock I will build my church, and the gates of Hades will not prevail against it. I will give you the keys of the kingdom of heaven, and whatever you bind on earth will be bound in heaven, and whatever you loose on earth will be loosed in heaven'" (Matthew 16:16-19).

Just as a mayor holds the keys to a city as a sign of his authority, Jesus uses "keys" as the symbol of the authority he gives to Peter. Peter and the eleven other apostles are the foundation of the only Church founded solely by Jesus Christ. Paul explains our personal bond with the apostolic foundation of the Church: "So then you are no longer strangers and aliens, but you are citizens with the saints and also members of the household of God, built upon the foundation of the apostles and prophets, with Christ Jesus himself as the cornerstone. In him the whole structure is joined together and grows into a holy temple in the Lord; in whom you also are built together spiritually into a dwelling place for God" (Ephesians 2:19-22).

The Church's foundation–such is the great dignity of the apostles whom we follow as we are built by our faith and action, as stone and mortar, into Jesus' Church.

Jesus chose Peter but Peter did not understand his role in the Church right away. After Jesus rose from the dead, he appeared to his disciples (who had gone fishing) and cooked breakfast for them on the beach.[51] That morning, Jesus made clear to Peter what was expected of him: "When they had finished breakfast, Jesus said to Simon Peter, 'Simon son of John, do you love me more than these?' He said to him, 'Yes, Lord; you know that I love you.' Jesus said to him, 'Feed my lambs.' A second time he said to him, 'Simon son of John, do you love me?' He said to him, 'Yes, Lord; you know that I love you.' Jesus said to him, 'Tend my sheep.' He said to him the third time, 'Simon son of John, do you love me?' Peter felt hurt because he said to him the third time, 'Do you love me?' And he said to him, 'Lord, you know everything; you know that I love you.' Jesus said to him, 'Feed my sheep'" (John 21:15-17). Three times Jesus told Peter to feed and care for his sheep. Most emphatically, Jesus urged Peter to accept God's Will and pick up the shepherd's staff. No more looking for fish! Seek out souls for the kingdom of God! And Peter, empowered by the Holy Spirit at Pentecost, did just that.

Jesus did not abandon his teachings to chaotic interpretations. He handpicked men who protected his Church's teachings and kept them free from error. These men knew Jesus; they lived with him, ate with him, walked many miles with him listening to the wonders of the kingdom of God, watched his interactions with people, and engaged him in casual conversation. They repeated not only his words but also his actions when they carried on his work. The apostle John wrote at the end of his Gospel, "But there are also many other things that Jesus did; if every one of them were written down, I suppose that the world itself could not contain the books that would be written" (John 21:25). As the Church grew in distant communities, Gospels and letters were written, and the words and the teachings that Jesus and the Holy Spirit gave to the apostles were codified as Christianity.

How important are the apostles in Jesus' plan of salvation? So important that they are the foundation of the eternal city we hope for: "And the wall of the city has twelve foundations, and on them are the twelve names of the twelve apostles of the Lamb" (Revelations 21:14).

Apostolic Succession

"… and the gates of Hades will not prevail against it" (Matthew 16:18). Jesus did not build a Church that collapsed when the apostles died. He guaranteed that his Church would carry on through an unbroken line of apostolic successors until the end of time. But the "gates of Hades" tries, often through weak or corrupt people, to destroy the Church. From the foundation of the Church, heretics have tried to distort Jesus' teachings. Some heretics are ignorant or misinformed, but some are self-serving liars. Here are a few examples:

The Jewish leaders, by their knowledge of prophecy, suspected that Jesus was the Messiah yet plotted to kill him even from his birth in Bethlehem, then plotted against his disciples.

Judas Iscariot, chosen to be an apostle, spent three years accompanying Jesus, teaching people about the coming of God's Kingdom, and performing miracles in Jesus' name. But he had a corrupt and sinful soul. Mary, the sister of Lazarus, poured expensive perfume on Jesus' feet and wiped them with her hair.[52] "But Judas Iscariot, one of his disciples (the one who was about to betray him), said, 'Why was this perfume not sold for three hundred denarii and the money given to the poor?' (He said this not because he cared about the poor, but because he was a thief; he kept the common purse and used to steal what was put into it.)" (John 12:4-6).

THE GRACE OF CHURCH

Judas' corruption caused him to lack understanding of the seriousness of sin, which resulted in grave sin in his soul. Judas' sinfulness caused him to choose to betray Jesus to the most heinous method of capital punishment known to the Roman Empire. Judas had a choice. The chief priests were plotting to kill Jesus, but Judas willingly made himself the instrument of Jesus' betrayal. Judas' hypocritical and heretical actions gave scandal to Jesus' followers and their faith was shaken.

Let us not forget the false prophets who confused the Galatians. Paul had to defend Christian teaching against men who claimed that the Galatians were not Christian because they had not converted to Judaism first. The "gates of Hades" began its war against the Church at its birth.

Paul warned the Colossians regarding their local heretics: "See to it that no one takes you captive through philosophy and empty deceit, according to human tradition, according to the elemental spirits of the universe, and not according to Christ." (Colossians 2:8). This warning is pertinent today, too!

God can turn any evil into good. Through his suffering, crucifixion, and resurrection, Jesus was the 'atoning sacrifice...for the sins of the world' (1 John 2:2), giving the human race a chance to confess their sins, ask God for forgiveness, and be healed. Because of Jesus' act of tremendous charity, God destroyed the condemnation of sin equaling hell. Our Father sacrificed his only begotten son to establish this covenant with humankind and give us this great healing.

Paul wrote to Timothy, "Avoid profane chatter, for it will lead people into more and more impiety, and their talk will spread like gangrene. Among them are Hymenaeus and Philetus[53], who have swerved from the truth by claiming the resurrection has already taken place. They are upsetting the faith of some" (2 Timothy 2:16-18). Hymenaeus and Philetus claimed that the resurrection occurred when souls were freed from sin at baptism and they denied a future bodily resurrection. Remember Arianism? Arias taught that Jesus is not God and not one with the Father. (Aquilina)

There are popular cults who profess similar heresies and misleadingly call themselves Christian. Their members knock on people's doors to convert the ignorant and unsuspecting to their heretical teachings.

Nestorianism separated Jesus' human and divine natures. Nestorius' errant teachings were condemned in 431 by the Council of Ephesus. (Chapman)

Sabellius' heresy taught there is no Trinity and God the Father came to earth as Jesus. (Aquilina)

Gnostics were intellectual elite cultists who believed all created things are intrinsically evil. They denied both the Trinity and the Incarnation of Jesus. (Aquilina)

And many other attacks on the Church Jesus founded, especially cults which insist that we can understand God. How illogical! How can we, imperfect as we are, understand God's perfection? We do not understand ourselves but they tell us we can understand God!? Sadly, false prophets are confusing well-meaning people with these and other heresies even to this day.

The above are all examples of the "gates of Hades" warring against the Truth Christ entrusted to his Church, but we have Christ's promise, the Church will prevail.

The writings of the early Church Fathers reveal their struggle for the faith and their zeal for the Church. Just as Paul worked diligently to keep the churches he founded from wandering off in their own directions or being led astray, so did the early Church Fathers. In 325 A.D., when the Council of Nicea was convened, there was no Bible as we know it. The Christian faithful relied on ordained bishops, who received their commission by virtue of apostolic succession, for the truth of the letters and writings that were read in the churches before the breaking of the bread. Other councils were convened when it became necessary to combat heresy and clarify teachings as the world changed. Through these gatherings, heretics and false prophets were prevented from perverting the Truth as Jesus taught it, and the Bible came to be.

The apostles, guided by the Holy Spirit, followed the example of Jesus. They anointed men as apostolic successors, called bishops, who followed, taught, and defended Christianity. No official Bible existed during the first few centuries of Christianity but the Gospels and other writings, recognized by the bishops as authoritative, were read in house churches in various cities before the breaking of the bread. The writings that were overwhelmingly deemed inspired became our New Testament.

When the apostles were gone, the bishops, through the power of the Holy Spirit, governed and defended Jesus' Church and preserved his words and example. Even though they lived in different cities during a time of Christian persecution, they wrote to and encouraged each other, and occasionally corrected one another's errors. The early Church Fathers, the bishops who came after the apostles, continued the fight against heresy and protected the apostolic Church. Faithful bishops continue this fight against the "gates of Hades" to this day.

Modern Christians do not properly appreciate the struggles and sufferings of the men who led the early Christian Church. War came to them on two fronts. How difficult it was to be Christian in a pagan world where Christians were the heretics, a crime punishable by horrendous torture and death! Many bishops and Christian men and women were martyred. It was made even more difficult to lead the Church as it was being attacked at the same time by heretics, the greedy wolves from within!

Reading the letters and writings of the early Church Fathers, like Polycarp, a disciple of John the Evangelist, and his disciple, Irenaeus of Lyons, as well as, Ignatius of Antioch, and many others, draws us closer to the faith, hope, love, and the passionate zeal for God that our early Church brothers and sisters demonstrated as they struggled to remain Christian in a pagan world. Familiarity and solidarity with the early Church gives today's Christians insight into what we truly believe, why we believe it, and makes us less likely to be swayed by superfluous argument, heresy, and distortion.

It was the willingness of the apostles and their successors to accept their calling that facilitated the great flow of graces God desired to send upon the Church. Just as the apostles answered Jesus' call to "Come, follow me," so the apostolic successors accepted the calling, followed Christ in the footsteps of his apostles, and became distributors of God's grace.

The Grace of Holy Priesthood

After God led the Israelites out of Egypt, he gave detailed instructions for a tabernacle, a meeting tent, to be built.[54] God instructed Moses, "Then bring near to you your brother Aaron, and his sons with him, from among the Israelites, to serve me as priests–Aaron and Aaron's sons, Nadab and Abihu, Eleazar and Ithamar" (Exodus 28:1). Exodus 28 describes in detail the symbolic and richly-appointed vestments God ordered made for his priests, signifying the great dignity of the priesthood. Then God instructed

Moses to anoint Aaron as high priest and to ordain Aaron's sons as priests; "...and the priesthood shall be theirs by perpetual ordinance..." (Exodus 29:9). Thus Aaron's sons ordained their sons, and so on, according to the Law God gave to Moses.

In the same way, Jesus chose his first twelve apostles and taught them the sublime truths of the kingdom of God. Jesus conferred the holy priesthood upon his apostles on the day of his Resurrection. The apostles ordained successors to carry out Jesus' commission. Those bishops ordained the next generation of bishops, and so on to this day. The methods for ordination have varied over the centuries but the minimum requirement is prayer and the laying of hands by an ordained bishop on the chosen man.[55] The only legitimate priesthood is through the lineage initiated by Jesus and the ordination of individuals outside of this holy line does not conform to Scripture. Religions that have strayed away from the Church Jesus founded lack the authority to ordain ministers of God. They lack the authority Christ gave to Peter. Consequently, there is little consistency in these religions, even among their own ranks. It is frequently up to individual pastors to interpret and teach the Gospels. Consequently, some Protestant religions have splintered into thousands of sects, and some have re-interpreted the Gospel so grossly that they can no longer be recognized as Christian. Given the factors that are missing, authority, consistency, and lineage, they are inadequate to meet the doctrines that our Lord and Savior gave to his apostles, despite all good intentions.

Even with the lineage and authority given to the universal Church, there are problems. Christian leaders, who betray Jesus and the faithful, teach heresy, use their positions to their own ends, and give bad example to their flocks, will have to answer to Justice. Jesus warned his disciples, "... 'Beware of the yeast of the Pharisees, that is, their hypocrisy. Nothing is covered up that will not be uncovered, and nothing secret that will not become known'" (Luke 12:1-2). The uncovering is currently ongoing. But, by the grace of God, faithful apostolic successors continue to guide the flock through difficult and changing times, as Jesus promised, "… the gates of Hades shall not prevail against it" (Matthew 16:18).

It is through the gifts received by the men ordained to the holy priesthood that special graces of God, Sacraments, are made available to us. Clergy ordained outside of the line of apostolic succession, have no more authority to administer Jesus' gifts of grace than a layperson.

The Grace of Baptism

After the Resurrection, Jesus appeared to his apostles and commissioned them, "Go therefore and make disciples of all nations, baptizing them in the name of the Father and of the Son and of the Holy Spirit, and teaching them to obey everything that I have commanded you" (Matthew 28:19-20). "And he said to them, 'Go into all the world and proclaim the good news to the whole creation. The one who believes and is baptized will be saved; but the one who does not believe will be condemned'" (Mark 16:15-16). Thus, Jesus gave the apostles their marching orders.

Jesus pronounced the formula for Baptism: "…in the name of the Father and of the Son and of the Holy Spirit" (Matthew 28:19). Leave out the Father - no baptism. Leave out the Son - no baptism. Leave out the Holy Spirit - no baptism. No Trinity - no baptism. Jesus revealed the Trinitarian nature of God to us when he lived among us. The Christian Church definitively proclaimed the Trinity at the Council of Nicea in 325 A.D. in the Nicene Creed. When an individual is baptized into the Christian Church, they are being baptized into the truths proclaimed in the Nicene Creed.

Why be baptized? Well, if because Jesus commanded it is not enough reason, here are additional reasons to accept this great grace God offers us:

Baptism is the initiation into Jesus' Church. After the disciples received the Holy Spirit at Pentecost, Peter made his first speech to a large crowd in

Jerusalem and testified that the crucified and risen Jesus was the Messiah. The crowd's reaction? "Now when they heard this, they were cut to the heart and said to Peter and to the other apostles, 'Brothers, what should we do?' Peter said to them, 'Repent, and be baptized every one of you in the name of Jesus Christ so that your sins may be forgiven; and you will receive the gift of the Holy Spirit.'" (Acts 2:37-38). "So those who welcomed his message were baptized, and that day about three thousand persons were added. They devoted themselves to the apostles' teaching and fellowship, to the breaking of the bread and the prayers" (Acts 2:41-42). By the grace of baptism, Christian life begins. Read Acts 2:14-36 for Peter's rousing speech to the crowd.

Baptism frees us from original sin and leaves a permanent spiritual mark on the soul. Just as the original sin of Adam and Eve marked human-kind as the property of Satan, so Baptism erases Satan's stain and marks us as children of God. Baptism is our "YES" to God's offer of forgiveness, our acknowledgement that Christ died to remove the sins of the world, and our acceptance of our share in his life, death and resurrection. "Do you not know that all of us who have been baptized into Christ Jesus were baptized into his death? Therefore, we have been buried with him by baptism into death, so that, just as Christ was raised from the dead by the glory of the Father, so we, too, might walk in newness of life" (Romans 6:3-4). Baptism restores us to grace and makes us new!

Baptism builds us into the body of Christ, no matter how diverse our cultures in the world or our spiritual gifts. Paul explains in 1 Corinthians 12:13, "For in the one Spirit we were all baptized into one body–Jews or Greeks, slaves or free–and we were all made to drink of one Spirit." The baptized are united in grace with each other through the Holy Spirit. All we have to do is pay attention to the inspirations of the Holy Spirit!

Baptism's grace enables us to offer sacrifices of prayer, praise, and action to God as prophets, speakers, and doers of the word of God, and makes us royal adopted children of God, brothers and sisters of our Lord and King, Jesus Christ.

John the Baptist said of Jesus, "I baptize you with water for repentance, but one who is more powerful than I is coming after me; I am not worthy to carry his sandals. He will baptize you with the Holy Spirit and fire" (Matthew 3:11). Why then was Jesus, who could not sin, baptized? "Then Jesus came from Galilee to John at the Jordan, to be baptized by him. John would have prevented him, saying, 'I need to be baptized by you, and do you come to me?' But Jesus answered him, 'Let it be so now; for it is proper for us in this way to fulfill all righteousness.' Then he consented. And when Jesus had been baptized, just as he came up from the water, suddenly the heavens were opened to him and he saw the Spirit of God descending like a dove and alighting on him. And a voice from heaven said, 'This is my Son, the Beloved, with whom I am well pleased'" (Matthew 3:13-17). Righteousness is conforming to the Will of God. Jesus' Baptism demonstrated his obedience to our Father and his unity with humankind.

In case of an emergency, when a person is in danger of death and desires to be baptized, a lay person may perform the Baptism by pouring water on the person and saying: "I baptize you in the name of the Father, and of the Son, and of the Holy Spirit."

The Grace of Confirmation

Confirmation is a grace that is sometimes misunderstood. Some Protestant Christians argue that it is unnecessary because we receive the Holy Spirit at Baptism. And so we do. But God's grace received at Confirmation empowers our Christian witness. In this post-Christian era when Jesus' teachings are being rejected and fewer and fewer people witness to God's Truth, this sign and gift of God's grace is even more necessary and relevant.

Case in point: Despite seeing Jesus after he had risen from the dead, Peter went back to fishing. Peter's heart was willing; but he lacked the strength to be an effective witness for Jesus. Before he ascended into heaven, Jesus told the wavering apostles: "But you will receive power when the Holy Spirit has come upon you; and you will be my witnesses in Jerusalem, in all Judea and Samaria, and to the ends of the earth" (Acts 1:8). The apostles and disciples prayed as they waited for the Holy Spirit in Jerusalem. "When the day of Pentecost had come, they were all together in one place. And suddenly from heaven there came a sound like the rush of a violent wind, and it filled the entire house where they were sitting. Divided tongues, as of fire, appeared among them, and a tongue rested on each of them. All of them were filled with the Holy Spirit and began to speak in other languages, as the Spirit gave them ability" (Acts 2:1-4). This grace confirmed the apostles and disciples in faith and gave them the strength to carry out their mission.

The roar of the wind attracted a crowd of Jewish pilgrims who had come to Jerusalem to celebrate the feast of Pentecost. Each pilgrim heard Peter and the apostles speaking in his/her native language. Some in the crowd were amazed at the miracle, others accused the disciples of being drunk, but Peter used the opportunity to tell the crowd about the crucified Messiah, Jesus Christ. The apostles suddenly became fearless witnesses, performed many miracles, trusted God when they were threatened and imprisoned by the same Sanhedrin that had crucified Jesus, and rejoiced to suffer as Jesus had suffered when they were flogged for continuing to speak out about Jesus. A few weeks earlier, the apostles, except for John, hid while Jesus was being crucified. What a difference the Holy Spirit makes!

The apostles understood that Confirmation in the Holy Spirit is separate and unique from the grace of Baptism. For example: "Now when the apostles at Jerusalem heard that Samaria had accepted the word of God, they sent Peter and John to them. The two went down and prayed for them that they might receive the Holy Spirit (for as yet the Spirit had not come upon any of them; they had only been baptized in the name of the Lord Jesus). Then Peter and John laid their hands on them, and they received the Holy Spirit" (Acts 8:14-17). Another example: Paul met a group of Christians in Ephesus who had not heard of the Holy Spirit. They had received the baptism of John the Baptist. Paul instructed them about Jesus Christ and they accepted baptism in the name of Jesus. After that, "When Paul laid his hands on them, the Holy Spirit came upon them, and they spoke in tongues and prophesied–" (Act 19:6). Also, Paul writes in his letter to the Hebrews about his disappointment that they were not progressing in Christian perfection and lists the basic Christian teachings: "…repentance from dead works and faith toward God, instructions about baptisms, laying on of hands, resurrection of the dead, and eternal judgment" (Hebrews 6:1-2). The terms "instructions about baptisms" and "laying on of hands" (Confirmation) show that they are not one grace, but two.

Confirmation "confirms" our Christian vocation and gives us the grace of Christian maturity and wisdom to use the gifts of the Holy Spirit we receive in Baptism so that we can become like the apostles, powerful witnesses for our Lord Jesus Christ. "In him (Jesus Christ) you also, when you had heard the word of truth, the gospel of your salvation, and had believed in him, were marked with the seal of the promised Holy Spirit; this is the pledge of our inheritance toward redemption as God's own people, to the praise of his glory" (Ephesians 1:13-14).

The Grace of Certainty That We Are Forgiven

"For we do not have a high priest who is unable to sympathize with our weaknesses, but we have one who in every respect has been tested as we are, yet without sin. Let us therefore approach the throne of grace with boldness, so that we may receive mercy and find grace to help in time of need" (Hebrews 4:15-16).

The grace of Baptism washes away all sin and our souls become dazzling white, pure, innocent, and holy. Unfortunately, we do not stay that way. We sin because of human weakness, and the guilt we feel when we offend God makes us unhappy. When we run away from God in sin, he wants to draw us back, forgive us, comfort us, give us wisdom and grace to avoid sin, and reconcile with us.

To receive forgiveness for their sins, the Israelite people approached God through their High Priest with sacrificial offerings. The High Priest offered the prescribed unblemished ram to God in sacrifice and the people were assured that their sins were forgiven because they had fulfilled the Law of God. We receive forgiveness by approaching Jesus through his apostolic successors, his ordained bishops and priests. Thus, in Jesus' precious grace of Reconciliation, we are assured of the forgiveness of our sins as the ancient Israelites were assured of God's forgiveness.

So where did this precious gift of grace come from? On the evening of Easter Sunday, Jesus appeared to his disciples who were hiding in a locked room. "Jesus said to them again, 'Peace be with you. As the Father has sent me, so I send you.' When he had said this, he breathed on them and said to them, 'Receive the Holy Spirit. If you forgive the sins of any, they are forgiven them; if you retain the sins of any, they are retained'" (John 20:21-23). Through those words, Jesus gave his disciples the power of the Holy Spirit to act as mediator between man and God in the forgiveness of sins.

The gift of forgiveness is not about judgment. Only Jesus will judge us. God loves us and does not want sin to separate us from him. Too often our trust in God's forgiveness is weak or we believe that our sins are too awful to be forgiven. The priest, by the grace bestowed upon him at his ordination as an apostolic successor, mediates for us. He listens to the promptings of the Holy Spirit and guides the soul in his care. He then prays the absolution, a definitive sign that all of the soul's sins are forgiven. Reconciliation is a grace granted by God whereby, through an apostolic successor, God forgives sins, enlightens the soul, and gives the peace, grace, and wisdom to avoid sin. If immediate absolution cannot be offered, such as when a person refuses to give up a serious ongoing sin, then the priest gives guidance toward achieving ultimate peace and reconciliation with God. What most often separates us from God's forgiveness is our pride, the sin that separated Satan from God. Confessing our sins to God's priest strikes directly at the heart of sin, our pride. This is the wisdom of God.

The Grace of the Breaking of the Bread

At the first Passover, God told the Israelites through Moses to choose one lamb per household and mark the doorposts and lintel with the lamb's blood. These sacrificial lambs were eaten by the Israelites at the first Passover. Those who obeyed God were protected from the plague sent against the pagan Egyptians. God commanded his people to celebrate Passover each year in remembrance of their rescue from Egypt.

The last Old Testament prophet, John the Baptist, cried out when he saw Jesus, "... 'Here is the Lamb of God who takes away the sin of the world!'" (John 1:29). Christians, who in faith do God's Will, are forgiven and freed from just punishment and will have eternal life. What does God will us to do? "...Jesus said to them, 'Very truly, I tell you, unless you eat the flesh of the Son of Man and drink his blood, you have no life in you. Those who eat my flesh and drink my blood have eternal life, and I will raise them up on the last day; for my flesh is true food and my blood is true drink. Those who eat my flesh and drink my blood abide in me, and I in them. Just as the living Father sent me, and I live because of the Father, so whoever eats me will live because of me. This is the bread that came down from heaven, not like that which your ancestors ate, and they died. But the one who eats this bread will live forever'" (John 6:53-58).

Jesus said, "I am the living bread that came down from heaven. Whoever eats of this bread will live forever; and the bread that I will give for the life of the world is my flesh" (John 6:51). As you can imagine, Jesus listeners were shocked and offended. "The Jews then disputed among themselves, saying 'How can this man give us his flesh to eat?" (John 6:52). Many disciples walked away feeling foolish and betrayed, and thinking that they had been listening to a crazy man. Jesus knew what they were thinking but he did not stop them. He did not explain further, nor did he say, "Don't go! I didn't mean it!" Jesus had spoken a truth beyond their understanding. He had asked for a leap of faith that would separate believers from those who were simply following a miracle working rock star around Israel and Judah. The meaning of Jesus' words did not become clear until the Last Supper, the first Eucharistic celebration.

At the Last Supper, the solemn Passover meal before he died, Jesus gave his apostles the ultimate gift, himself, and instructions to share his gift. "Then he took a loaf of bread, and when he had given thanks, he broke it and gave it to them, saying, 'This is my body, which is given for you. Do this in remembrance of me.' And he did the same with the cup after supper, saying, 'This cup that is poured out for you is the new covenant in my blood'" (Luke 22:19-20).

By his own Will in his Divinity, and out of obedience to God our Father in his humanity, Jesus gave his life as the sacrificial Lamb of Passover. He gave us his true Body to eat and his true Blood to drink in the form of bread and wine, just as he, the truly Divine Son of God, took the form of our human flesh at his Incarnation.

There was much debate at the beginning of the Protestant movement regarding the words of Jesus, "This is my body." Believe it or not, the debate pretty much boiled down to the definition of the word "is." Some early Protestant theologians, like Martin Luther, argued that the word "is" means **is**, while others argued that "is" means something like "represents" or, the wishy-washy "it is but it isn't." The definition of the word "is," in this context, is a debate among Christians that is ongoing today. Sadly, this means that many Christians deny the "true food" and the "true drink" and the promise Jesus made that, "Those who eat my flesh and drink my blood have eternal life, and I will raise them up on the last day" (John 6:54).

The Grace of Healing

"Then Jesus summoned his twelve disciples and gave them authority over unclean spirits, to cast them out, and to cure every disease and every sickness" (Matthew 10:1).

Jesus healed people wherever he went and instructed his apostles to imitate him: "As you go, proclaim the good news, 'The kingdom of heaven has come near.' Cure the sick, raise the dead, cleanse the lepers, cast out demons" (Matthew 10:7). Jesus gave his apostles the gift of healing. This gift of healing the sick continues in his Church by means of apostolic succession. "Are any among you sick? They should call for the elders of the church and have them pray over them, anointing them with oil in the name of the Lord" (James 5:14).

The Grace of Marriage

In the beginning, the very first relationship is between God and man. The second is between man and woman. In the most magnificent marriage ceremony of all time, with the choirs of angels as witnesses, the Lord God, as Father of the Bride, gave woman to man and they became "one flesh." This is the grace of marriage: the grace to act in union with one another, the grace to cooperate with God in creating children, and the grace to increase in love by growing closer in relationship to each other and to God.

The grace to act in union with one another: The character of marriage is relationship. It is not about self, but is other-centered. Acting in union with another human being is living the fullness of Christian charity. Holy marriage is humankind's most important vocation, and the greatest gift of God's grace. It is the foundation of humankind's physical continuation and its spiritual and moral culture. God holds the grace of marriage in such high honor that the book of Revelation compares the relationship of union between Jesus and his victorious Church to a marriage celebration. John writes:

"Then I heard what seemed to be the voice of a great multitude, like the sound of many waters and like the sound of mighty thunder-peals, crying out,

Hallelujah!

For the Lord our God the Almighty reigns.

Let us rejoice and exult and give him the glory,

for the marriage of the Lamb has come, and his bride is has made herself ready;

to her it has been granted to be clothed with fine linen, bright and pure' –

for the fine linen is the righteous deeds of the saints.

And the angel said to me, 'Write this:

Blessed are those who are invited to the marriage supper of the Lamb...'"

(Revelation 19:6-9).

Married men and women are called to a holiness that is difficult to comprehend and impossible to achieve without the grace God gives in the union of marriage.

The grace to act in cooperation with God in creating and educating children: God gives the gift of a child. The creative act between a husband and wife gives the physical body, through the grace of God. "For it was you who formed my inward parts; you knit me together in my mother's womb. I praise you, for I am fearfully and wonderfully made" (Psalm 139:13-14). God alone gives the child its soul, its human spirit, its life. There is no such thing as an unplanned child because all children fit into God's plan.

Accepting the creative gift of children is the greatest work that human beings can perform. Parents give their lives to God through raising children. There is no greater sacrifice of love that human beings can offer God than raising the children God places in their charge, no matter how the children come into their charge. The marriage grace to cooperate with God in creating and educating children is the primary means God has chosen to share his love with humankind.

The grace to increase in love by growing closer to each other and to God: How much damage errant human wills have done to the grace of marriage! If a married couple centers their lives on loving God, they put self-interest aside, generously accept the gift of children, and work together toward what is best for their family. Through cooperation with God's grace, the battle that original sin began between man and woman disappears. What Adam and Eve enjoyed in Paradise was a close, loving relationship with God. "...God is love, and those who abide in love abide in God, and God abides in them" (1 John 4:16). God is the only source of love. Therefore, if a husband and wife desire the loving relationship inherent in the marriage vows, God must be involved! In the waters of marital grace, husband and wife must swim together with God as their leader. Without God, there are no waters of marital grace and the fish flip and flop around, flopping into each other, without direction.

The importance of married love cannot be overly emphasized. Indeed, marital love is the cradle of all social justice. The quality of love between

a man and a woman determines the quality of love their children experience–generous true love or self-centered and manipulative behavior
masquerading as love. Betrayal of love teaches children mistrust. Children
who learn mistrust in their families have difficulty trusting God. God is
betrayed and social justice becomes perverted.

The Holy Temple

Jesus offers us these seven sacramental graces through his Church to
give Christians spiritual and physical strength, and to increase the soul's
virtue and understanding of God's Will. He asks for our cooperation to
receive these gifts of grace because he knows our human nature. So God
waits for us to acknowledge our needs and accept the gifts of grace he has
offered us all along. Through these sacramental graces, God offers us a
participation in Heavenly life and guides us to Jesus in the "inner shrine
behind the curtains."

CHAPTER 9

Christianity as Enigma

....

"And war broke out in heaven; Michael and his angels fought against the dragon. The dragon and his angels fought back, but they were defeated, and there was no longer any place for them in heaven. The great dragon was thrown down, that ancient serpent, who is called the Devil and Satan, the deceiver of the whole world—he was thrown down to the earth, and his angels were thrown down with him" (Revelation 12:7-9).

Good vs. Evil as Enigma

The ancient battle between Truth and deception, good and evil, continues and we are spiritual combatants. There is no "4F"[56] classification in spiritual warfare. Everybody fights. Evil attacks are devious, coming so stealthily that we become accustomed to an evil, even thinking it is good, until the horror of the evil's consequences shocks us back to Truth. The devil is a master at manipulation. He makes lies seem reasonable. To defeat him, we must understand his deceptive tactics. It is time for a history lesson:

The Third Reich. After World War I, the German people suffered serious economic hardships. The Treaty of Versailles imposed severe war reparation fines upon Germany and required that the German people elect a democratic government, an unfamiliar system of governance for a people accustomed to monocracy. The disastrous result was high unemployment and a ruinous currency devaluation that impoverished the angry and frustrated German people. It was at this time that Adolph Hitler, a charismatic speaker and a man with a plan, began community organizing in Bavaria. He saw opportunity in the misery of the German people. A master at propaganda, he directed their desire for change to his political advantage. So began the Nazi Party and the horrors of World War II (Shirer).

The world was warned. Hitler was arrested in his community organizing days and sentenced to prison. He used this time to write a book, Mein Kampf, which clearly set out his philosophy and plan of action: Germans were a superior race. All other races existed to serve the German people. Jews were lesser human beings, inconvenient, and could be exterminated without consequence (Shirer).

As a young adult, Hitler lived a hand-to-mouth existence in Vienna while he pursued his interest in art. During those days, he observed the inner workings of political movements, particularly one very successful political movement that used propaganda to manipulate public opinion. He wrote in Mein Kampf:

"I understood the infamous spiritual terror which this movement exerts, particularly on the bourgeoisie, which is neither morally nor mentally equal to such attacks; at a given sign it unleashes a veritable barrage of lies and slanders against whatever adversary seems most dangerous, until the nerves of the attacked persons break down... This is a tactic based on precise calculation of all human weaknesses, and its result will lead to success with almost mathematical certainty...

I achieved an equal understanding of the importance of physical terror toward the individual and the masses... For while in the ranks of their supporters the victory achieved seems a triumph of the justice of their own cause, the defeated adversary in most cases despairs of the success of any further resistance" (Shirer).

Using this formula, Adolph Hitler slandered his enemies, and deceived and terrorized the German people into pursuing his goal of Nazi world domination. He made speeches telling the people what they wanted to hear, and then did whatever he pleased, unleashing a "veritable barrage of lies and slanders" against anyone who dared to challenge his absolute authority. He manipulated facts with such mastery and boldness that his lies became the people's truth. Hitler wrote in Mein Kampf, "The crowd will remember only the simplest concepts repeated a thousand times." This is the formula of the devil, the father of lies.

Hitler set his sights on absolute power in Germany, but Hitler was not German. He was born in Austria. That fact made him ineligible to run for the German presidency. However, Hitler would not be deterred by facts. He arranged for a Nazi friend from the state of Brunswick to appoint him as attaché to the legation from Brunswick to Berlin. The appointment automatically made him a German citizen. But there had never before been a legation from Brunswick to Berlin. The appointment was a deception. Hitler then used his formula to be elected Chancellor of Germany. The day before German President, Field Marshall von Hindenburg died, Hitler's handpicked cabinet made a law that joined the offices of the President and the Chancellor into one. The law was unconstitutional but those with the authority to stop the charade were terrified by Hitler's violent rhetoric and brutal dealings. Hitler effectively became German dictator and his ruthless Nazi agenda became law (Shirer). Hitler came to power by lies, deception, and violence, and the populace closed its eyes because Hitler's agenda was deemed "good" by the populace.

One of Hitler's lesser-publicized agendas was to eliminate Christianity because Jesus threatened his Nazi Socialism. Since most Germans considered themselves Christian, Hitler could not ban Christianity outright, so he decided to realign Christian doctrine to suit his Nazi Socialist doctrine. He appointed his friend, Ludwig Muller, a former Navy Chaplain, as Reich

Bishop. Muller unified all of the Protestant churches under one umbrella church, the Protestant Reich Church. Muller was a Nazi, a heretic, and an anti-Semite. And Jesus was a Jew. You can see the problem.

To ensure that Christians were indoctrinated in Nazi state religious propaganda, Muller rewrote the Bible! In Reich theology, Jesus was an Aryan who fought against the Jews. The only Christianity allowed was the Reich version. Dissenting Christians were threatened with loss of their social status and livelihood, concentration camp living, or death. The initial reaction of Christians was shock and confusion, but Hitler unleashed a "veritable barrage of lies and slanders" against those who opposed Reich theology. Many Germans acquiesced. Some courageous Protestant dissidents formed the Confessional Church to defy Nazi propaganda and the takeover of the Protestant Churches. The Catholic Church defied Hitler in public letters and by protecting Hitler's enemies. Many priests and nuns were arrested. Hitler's Nazi government used a "veritable barrage of lies and slanders" to justify seizing the property of dissenting organizations, including Catholic schools, hospitals, orphanages, and universities, turning them into centers for Hitler's youth indoctrination and other Nazi institutions (Shirer).

"First they came for..."[7] The quality of a nation can be defined by its religious tolerance. The freedom a government allows its citizens to worship God without interference is a good sign of the quality of the freedom that nation has to offer. Freedom of conscience is the right to follow one's own beliefs in matters of religion and morality (Oxford Living Dictionaries). Government suppression of religious freedom has brought about the mass exodus of peoples, from the great Exodus led by Moses to the present-day flight of Christians from Middle Eastern countries.

Sadly, even in so-called free countries, citizens are not free. Christians in the United States of America suffer religious persecution even though a provision in the Constitution of the United States' Bill of Rights clearly states, "Congress shall make no law respecting an establishment of religion, or prohibiting the free exercise thereof." For example:

The U.S. Congress passed the Patient Protection and Affordable Care Act (ACA) that was touted as good and necessary to make healthcare available to all citizens, but provisions in this law are deceitful. This law redefines pregnancy prevention, abortion pills, and voluntary surgical abortion as necessary "healthcare." It mandates that employers provide this "healthcare" for their employees regardless of their moral beliefs. Churches are exempt from this "healthcare" requirement but church operated institutions–schools, hospitals, orphanages, nursing homes, and universities– must buy abortion insurance coverage for their employees or face crippling tax penalties. For example: The law requires Catholic nursing homes run by nuns to provide abortion and pregnancy prevention insurance coverage for all of their employees, in spite of the Church's vehement opposition to abortion and unnatural pregnancy prevention, or face fines that would close these institutions, even if the employees do not want the coverage! Legislated compromise to relieve these organizations from having to pay directly for abortion insurance involves hypocritical acceptance of an immoral law. Voluntary abortion is abhorrent to Christians.

Christian business owners must choose between obedience to God and obedience to the U.S. government! But, what is the cost of preserving a good conscience in the United States? Christians who resist ACA's onerous provisions must file lawsuits in court, pay burdensome legal fees, and are threatened with heavy tax penalties, and the possible loss of their businesses. They face the expensive and oppressive burden of a legal battle against the United States Government's never ending supply of lawyers, interminable court dates, and convoluted burdens of proof. They face a "veritable barrage of lies and slanders" for holding to God's Truth. The process is discouraging and financially impossible for average citizens.

The United States government, under the pretext of making healthcare available to all its citizens, has made a law "respecting the establishment" of a secular religion and "prohibiting the free exercise" of Christianity. The United States government has imposed a decidedly anti-Christian state belief system. Shall we call it "Secularity?" The elected government of the U.S.A. has effectively declared war upon Christians! Ironically, this is happening in a country where most of its citizens, even the same elected officials, claim to be Christian. This is madness!

How could this happen? "The crowd will remember only the simplest concepts repeated a thousand times." Corruptors' propaganda has made unborn human beings—the most helpless of all human beings—sacrifices to the secular gods of money, expediency, and convenience. Unborn people are now considered lesser human beings, inconvenient, and can be exterminated without consequence.

Why do some countries have a culture of "rights" supporting unnatural abortion? To understand, we can again look at why so many Germans supported Adolf Hitler. When Hitler campaigned for the position of German Chancellor, he appealed to the patriotism of German citizens and promised to rebuild Germany upon the foundation of the Christian Churches. He promised work for the unemployed, the restoration of financial stability, and the restoration of Christian values. What Christian would not support such promises? However, Hitler's agenda was clearly stated in Mein Kampf and people knew that the Nazi Party violently discouraged its rivals. Germans wanted to believe Hitler's false promises and overlooked the warning signs. They placed their faith in Adolph Hitler and accepted the Nazi agenda, which included the elimination of "undesirable" members of society: the Jews, the disabled, homosexuals, gypsies, and anyone who disagreed with Nazi Socialism—all scapegoats for Germany's woes. Eliminating undesirables was part of Hitler's agenda to improve the life of the average German citizen, just as the populace today believes that voluntary abortion of unborn human beings will improve the economic and personal lives of women and the citizenry in general, who will not have to support undesired or disabled children. Worldwide, organizations that promote abortion have various governments funding the exportation of this evil. Any group who opposes their propaganda is accused of cruelty toward women and the disabled, and is attacked with a "veritable barrage of lies and slanders."

The battle continues. The above is just a sample of Satan's battle tactics. Humans who choose to live without God are defenseless, but God protects and prepares his children for the fight. Understand this! Choose God or choose Satan! There is no neutral ground. The lukewarm and spiritually lazy are not innocent! Inaction against evil is a tacit nod of approval. Complacency allows evil to act freely. There are only two choices! Are you a soldier for God or one of Satan's minions?

At the beginning of the Church, Christians had to live their faith in a decidedly pagan world. Their lives were difficult. They were accused of everything from heresy against the pagan gods, to treason against Caesar, to cannibalism![58] They encouraged each other in their communities and the power of the Holy Spirit kept them united in the Faith. In the strength of unity, they withstood the pagan onslaught, and Christianity survived three hundred years of persecution before Constantine legalized it.

The early Christians knew their enemy. Paul warned, "Finally, be strong in the Lord and in the strength of his power. Put on the whole armor of God, so that you may be able to stand against the wiles of the devil. For our struggle is not against enemies of blood and flesh, but against the rulers, against the authorities, against the cosmic powers of this present darkness, against the spiritual forces of evil in the heavenly places" (Ephesians 6:10-12). Our battle is also against the "powers of this present darkness" and the "spiritual forces of evil." Christian life is spiritual warfare. Jesus fought against Satan his entire life, running from Herod as an infant, being tempted in the desert, being vilified by corrupt Temple authorities, being betrayed by Judas, and being crucified. He battled evil constantly. Should we expect differently?

The enigma? Why do Christians put on "the whole armor of God" if Jesus has already won the battle? Spiritual warfare results in the growth of virtue in our souls. When a soul rejects temptation, its virtue grows. Acts of rejecting temptation are spiritual fertilizer. However unpleasant they may seem, they make the flowers of virtue grow. We should be thankful for the suffering of spiritual battles since they bring us closer to eternal joy. Spiritual warfare will not end until Jesus returns in glory as the Just Judge, so take advantage of these opportunities to battle temptation and grow closer to God.

God provides the armor but we must bring something to the battle: our efforts to grow in virtue. As we make efforts to practice virtue, God grants us graces that increase our virtue. The stronger we grow in virtue, the more effective we will be in the fight. It doesn't hurt to pray for the virtues. God answers the prayers of souls who desire to grow closer to him.

What are the virtues? They are: "... the fruit of the Spirit is love, joy, peace, patience, kindness, generosity, faithfulness, gentleness, and self-control..." (Galatians 5:22-23). "And now faith, hope, and love abide, these three; and the greatest of these is love" (1 Corinthians 13:13). From the Ten Commandments: reverence for God, fear of the Lord, worship, praise and gratitude toward God, obedience, honor, charity, respect, temperance, justice, chastity, honesty, moderation and prudence, and from the Beatitudes: patient endurance, fortitude, humility, righteousness, courage, and mercy.

The seeds of virtue are planted at Baptism. They increase as we pursue holiness of life. Humility is the foundation for all virtue. Souls lacking humility refuse to acknowledge that they need God and block the actions of the Holy Spirit. The other virtues, firmly grounded in humility, form the structure. Faith, hope, fortitude, and gratitude to God are corner posts. The roof is the virtue of obedience, from which comes wisdom. Charity is the "glue" that connects, completes, and fortifies all virtue, and holds the entire structure together. Without charity, there can be no virtue. Virtue is our fortress against the "powers of this present darkness" and the "spiritual forces of evil."

"Stand therefore, and fasten the belt of truth around your waist, and put on the breastplate of righteousness. As shoes for your feet put on whatever will make you ready to proclaim the gospel of peace. With all of these, take the shield of faith, with which you will be able to quench all the flaming arrows of the evil one. Take the helmet of salvation, and the sword of the Spirit, which is the word of God" (Ephesians 6:14-17). And remember, we have assurance of final victory!

God's Justice Is Enigma

Human beings sin so we must face God's just judgment. We all do things that offend God and neighbor. Every human being on earth is a sinner. Souls who ignore the light of Wisdom, Jesus, place themselves in danger of spiritual death. And, it gets worse. Once souls lose God's light, they cannot stop sinning. They wander around in the darkness, confused, and unable to help themselves. They need God's justice. When Adam and Eve sinned, they lost the preternatural gifts they had enjoyed. But what about the larger consequences of Adam and Eve's actions, the loss of humankind to Satan? The repair of that damage and the payment of that debt were beyond the ability of Adam and Eve. Only God's justice can repair the damage done by sin.

What is God's justice? Sin cannot enter Heaven. God sent his Divine Son to be crucified and thereby pay the debt for our sins. Jesus suffered crucifixion to redeem each one of us. He paid off the debt of our sin and freed our souls to enter Heaven. Try to comprehend the debt we owe Jesus for the gift of our redeemed souls! Understand the immense value God places on every human life! Why can't we see that immense value in each other?

On the night he was betrayed, Jesus prayed for the apostles and for each of us: "I ask not only on behalf of these, but also on behalf of those who will believe in me through their word, that they may all be one. As you, Father, are in me and I am in you, may they also be in us, so that the world may believe that you have sent me" (John 17:20-21). Jesus prayed that night for each one of us to be "in" God. God desires an intimate, loving, personal, spiritual relationship "in" him for each of us! Jesus prayed to our Father that we, the creatures who had sinned against him, might share God's glory! Imagine, sharing in the glory of God! That is our loving God's justice for us. We are now God's adopted children—if we choose to be.

God's choice for us is mercy. Our challenge is to practice the virtue of humility and accept God's mercy. We must acknowledge and regret our sinfulness with our whole hearts, have faith in Jesus as our Savior and love God and neighbor. Faith in Jesus as our Savior guides us to where we belong: living "in" God's love and "in" God's will.

Accepting Jesus as our Savior demands an active commitment to God's work. We cannot just say, "Jesus, I accept you as my Savior," and go on our way as before in our sin. Paul the apostle calls the Christian people "the body of Christ."[59] If we are not required by love to be active in our commitment to Jesus, why do we need to be a body? We must act as members of the Christian community to do God's work on earth. When Paul heard of the great faith in the Christian community at Colossae, he wrote to them: "For this reason, since the day we heard it, we have not ceased praying for you and asking that you may be filled with the knowledge of God's will in all spiritual wisdom and understanding, so that you may lead lives worthy of the Lord, fully pleasing to him, as you bear fruit in every good work and as you grow in the knowledge of God" (Colossians1:9-10). Good works, done out of love for God, help us to grow in knowledge of God and draw us closer to God's supreme love and to our goal of eternal life with him. The immensity of God's love cannot be described in earthly terms; there are no human words or concepts to describe his desire to share his love and eternal life with us.

How is it then that some will be thrown, "... into the outer darkness, where there will be weeping and gnashing of teeth" (Matthew 25:30)? Simply put, in his justice, God gave us a free will. God's love is freely chosen. We may (1), choose to love God, obey his Will, and enjoy his gift of eternal happiness, or (2), acknowledge God but choose to remain lukewarm, follow any number of our own interests or false gods, and reject God's mercy, or (3), choose to make ourselves gods by denying God altogether. Choices two and three risk "the outer darkness, where there will be weeping and gnashing of teeth" (Matthew 25:30).

The soul chooses its afterlife, heaven or hell. God loves us, gives us many opportunities to know him, and is always nearby, waiting, even to our final breath, so that we might choose his mercy. God will not make souls accept eternal happiness. Eternity is the choice of a free will. At the time of death, a soul already knows where it will spend eternity because it has freely chosen its destination. Its only hope is to beg for forgiveness and Divine mercy.

Death is Enigma

Our idea of death and God's definition of death are not the same. At baptism, we die with Christ and are raised again with him, freed from all sin, including the legal claim of original sin that Satan holds against us. "When you were buried with him (Christ)[60] in baptism, you were also raised with him through faith in the power of God, who raised him from the dead" (Colossians 2:12). "So if you have been raised with Christ, seek the things that are above, where Christ is, seated at the right hand of God.

Set your minds on things that are above, not on things that are on earth, for you have died, and your life is hidden with Christ in God. When Christ who is your life is revealed, then you also will be revealed with him in glory" (Colossians 3:1-4). We are alive in God's grace when we are "hidden with Christ in God."

We have to die to this world to become part of the body of Christ and we do this dying while we are still breathing and walking around! We are dead to the ways of a world that do not put God first. We are still going to work, buying groceries, paying taxes, etc. but we do these things as children of God, in hope, as future citizens of heaven. The transient nature of our current situation puts our daily existence in perspective. Christ is with us, Christ is in us, we are the body of Christ! We can endure anything in Christ. This does not mean life will be easy, but it means that in Christ, we have all that we need to cope. We have the wisdom and peace of Christ and we are never alone. We will suffer; there will still be illness, tragedy, and disaster. Salvation history is not yet complete.

"Your life is hidden with Christ in God." Our sufferings are "hidden with Christ." Our joys, prayers, and good works are "hidden with Christ." Nothing is wasted. Every moment of our lives is important for salvation, and just as Christ's sufferings redeemed us, we participate in salvation history by dying in baptism and living "hidden with Christ." The death of our bodies is not so traumatic if we have already died to the world. We will leave behind the material means we used to do God's will because we do not need them anymore. Our spirits will fly home to our loving God and we will await the resurrection of our new and glorious bodies. To the Christian living in God's love, physical death brings us to our ultimate goal: God, himself.

By contrast, souls who reject God's grace are very anxious about the things of the world. Their souls are dead in sin. Their only hope lies in running to God's mercy.

The Holy Trinity Is Enigma

Christianity recognizes three Divine Persons in one God, our Creator Father, Jesus, his co-equal Son and our Redeemer, and the Holy Spirit, our Sanctifier, co-equal with the Father and the Son whom we receive at Baptism. The Holy Spirit was revealed by Jesus who said, "But the Advocate, the Holy Spirit, whom the Father will send in my name, will teach you everything, and remind you of all that I have said to you" (John 14:26). The Holy Spirit spoke to the apostles and disciples, guiding them in their missionary work.[61] He is not a "force" but a person with whom we can develop a relationship, like our Father and Jesus. The Holy Spirit speaks to us, too.

Any religion that denies the Trinitarian nature of God denies what has been revealed to us by Jesus and the apostles, and lacks the fullness of truth. They deny God his true identity. God is three distinct persons in one. Jesus revealed God's Trinitarian nature to us as he spoke: "When the Spirit of truth comes, he will guide you into all the truth; for he will not speak on his own, but will speak whatever he hears, and he will declare to you the things that are to come. He will glorify me, because he will take what is mine and declare it to you. All that the Father has is mine. For this reason I said that he will take what is mine and declare it to you" (John 16:13-15). The Spirit is as privy to the great mysteries and wisdom of the Father as is Jesus. They share a mysterious and unique oneness as God while also maintaining their unique individualities as the Father, Son, and the Holy Spirit. The Father, Son, and Holy Spirit, the Holy Trinity, is the perfection of oneness in love as family and in relationship.

Trinitarian action was revealed to the Virgin Mary by the Archangel Gabriel who said to Mary, "'And now, you will conceive in your womb and bear a son, and you will name him Jesus. He will be great, and will be called the Son of the Most High, and the Lord God will give to him the throne of his ancestor David. He will reign over the house of Jacob forever, and of his kingdom there will be no end.' Mary said to the angel, 'How can this be, since I am a virgin?' The angel said to her, 'The Holy Spirit will come upon you, and the power of the Most High will overshadow you; therefore, the child to be born will be holy; he will be called Son of God'" (Luke 1:31-35). There was Trinitarian participation in the mysterious conception of Jesus in Mary's virginal womb.

Trinitarian action was revealed at the Baptism of Jesus. After Jesus was baptized, "… suddenly the heavens were opened to him and he saw the Spirit of God descending like a dove and alighting on him. And a voice from heaven said, 'This is my Son, the Beloved, with whom I am well pleased'" (Matthew 3:16-17). After his resurrection, Jesus told his disciples, "Go therefore and make disciples of all nations, baptizing them in the name of the Father and of the Son and of the Holy Spirit" (Matthew 28:19). These words, revealing the Trinitarian nature of God, were spoken by Jesus himself. All four Gospels testify to Jesus' Trinitarian revelations. At that precise point in time, it pleased God to reveal his true nature to humankind. What an amazing time of grace in salvation history!

The Greatest Enigma The above are a few of the scriptures where God's nature is revealed. However, the Trinitarian nature of God is a matter of faith, not understanding. We have all eternity to contemplate God as Trinity as we enjoy our inheritance. The greatest enigma in all Christianity is the Trinitarian nature of our loving God.

CHAPTER 10

Suffering with Jesus

"For God so loved the world that he gave his only Son, so that everyone who believes in him may not perish but may have eternal life" (John 3:16).

See His Love for You!

Jesus obediently accepted his passion and death out of love for our Father and for us. He told the Pharisees and all within hearing distance, "I am the good shepherd. I know my own and my own know me, just as the Father knows me and I know the Father. And I lay down my life for the sheep. For this reason the Father loves me, because I lay down my life in order to take it up again. No one takes it from me, but I lay it down of my own accord. I have power to lay it down, and I have power to take it up again. I have received this command from my Father" (John 10:14-15, 17-18). No one made Jesus die for us. He did it for love.

Jesus constantly demonstrated his love in his straightforward actions. When the wedding couple in Cana ran out of wine, Jesus turned water into wine because his mother mentioned their dilemma to him. This miracle saved the young couple from social embarrassment, and "...his disciples believed in him" (John 2:11). If the crowds that followed him grew hungry, he fed them, while he invited them to partake of the "living water," the grace of God, refreshment that would never fail. Jesus freed souls trapped by demons, healed the sick, raised the dead, and revealed the secrets of God's Kingdom to all who would listen. He sent out his disciples to villages and towns to perform miracles and share the good news of the Kingdom of God; God, who gives hope, who promises eternal life, who loves, forgives, and heals. Jesus asks us to follow his example of self-sacrifice. Jesus tells us, "As the Father has loved me, so I have loved you; abide in my love. If you keep my commandments, you will abide in my love, just as I have kept my Father's commandments and abide in his love. I have said these things to you so that my joy may be in you, and that your joy may be complete. This is my commandment, that you love one another as I have loved you. No one has greater love than this, to lay down one's life for one's friends" (John 15:9-13).

When you read the Gospels about Jesus' arrest, do you see his suffering or his love for you? At the scourging, do you see his bloodied body or his love for you? At the crowning with thorns and the horrific crucifixion, do you see his love for you? Sometimes it is difficult to get past the horrific cruelty of Jesus' crucifixion and see his love, but love was his purpose. Not the common or shallow love represented by the world, but the depths of the love of God.

Share His Love for You!

Jesus did not suffer alone. "And she gave birth to her firstborn son and wrapped him in bands of cloth, and laid him in a manger, because there was no place for them in the inn" (Luke 2:7). A decree of Roman Emperor Augustus to take a census of all persons in his empire sent Mary and Joseph on a difficult journey to register in Joseph's ancestral home town of Bethlehem. Jesus was the "son of David" foretold in Scripture, and the fulfillment of God's promise to David meant that the Messiah would be born in the city of David—Bethlehem.

Mary and Joseph were the first human beings asked to suffer with Jesus. To help fulfill God's promise, they made a seventy-mile trip over rough terrain from Nazareth to Bethlehem. Joseph looked for lodging in an inn. He must not have had any friends or family in the area who could offer them a place to stay. How they must have suffered when all they could offer their newborn son was a cold, unpleasant stable for his first home and an animal's feeding trough for his first bed! Mary and Joseph cooperated with God's Will, no matter the cost, to fulfill God's plan for their newborn son. Jesus did not suffer alone for the salvation of humankind.

Soon after, Mary and Joseph were asked to suffer with Jesus again. The wicked Herod learned of the newborn King from the Magi and ordered the death of every child under the age of two in Bethlehem. An angel woke Joseph in the dead of night to warn him, and the Holy Family fled into Egypt.[62] How they must have suffered on the long journey, fearful of the danger to their son and horrified at the barbarity of Herod's army! How great was the horror and grief of the parents who lost their children and the shock of the entire community, which was powerless to stop Herod! Jesus did not suffer alone for the salvation of humankind.

How difficult it was for Joseph to support his family in Egypt, a country with a foreign language and culture. They could not take much with them from Bethlehem, so Mary had to re-establish their home enduring the same difficulties while caring for a small child. Jesus did not suffer alone for the salvation of humankind.

Jesus' parents were not the only people who suffered with him. Consider the disciples who left their businesses and families to follow Jesus, to endure the poverty and discomfort of walking endlessly in the heat and cold of the desert, from town to town, to help Jesus proclaim the good news of the Kingdom of God. They accepted Jesus' invitation to suffer with him. Consider the women who supported Jesus and who suffered with him at the foot of the cross. Consider Mary whose heart was pierced by a sword for love of her son. She remained with Jesus throughout his passion and death. Jesus' mother and the holy women accepted Jesus invitation to suffer with him. Jesus invited them to share his life, his sufferings, and his death as a prerequisite to the glory of eternal life. They believed in Jesus, hoped in his Word, and suffered with Jesus because they loved him.

Everywhere he went, Jesus invited the crowds to share his suffering. "He called the crowd with his disciples, and said to them, 'If any want to become my followers, let them deny themselves and take up their cross and follow me.'" (Mark 8:34). What a horrifying invitation! No one in his or her right mind would pick up a cross voluntarily. Those who picked up the cross were crucified! Yet thousands of people came to him. They brought the sick, and the sick of heart and soul to be healed. He comforted them, teaching them the Beatitudes, and telling them about God's justice, mercy, and loving-kindness.

Jesus spoke publicly in the Temple. His love for his Father and humankind was infinitely more important to him than preserving his worldly reputation or even his life. Jesus challenged the hypocrisy of the powerful Jewish leaders as they conspired to kill him and end his influence. It was dangerous to be a follower of Jesus and his disciples were afraid. "They were on the road, going up to Jerusalem, and Jesus was walking ahead of them; they were amazed, and those who followed were afraid. He took the twelve aside again and began to tell them what was to happen to him, saying, 'See, we are going up to Jerusalem, and the Son of Man will be handed over to the chief priests and the scribes, and they will condemn him to death; then they will hand him over to the Gentiles; they will mock him, and spit upon him, and flog him, and kill him; and after three days he will rise again.'" (Mark 10:32-34). Another time he told them, "Then they will hand you over to be tortured and will put you to death, and you will be hated by all nations because of my name'" (Matthew 24:9). Jesus made clear the sacrifice and suffering that following him would require. Jesus did not suffer alone for the salvation of humankind.

Loving Jesus

Suffering ranks with death as one of life's common denominators. Suffering communicates from person to person, country to country, and culture to culture, and God chose suffering to bring about the salvation of humankind. If we choose to suffer with Jesus, our suffering becomes productive, actually useful. It educates us, opens our eyes, and perfects our souls and those around us. It exposes hard-hearted and self-serving souls and softens them. It is useful for salvation. Graces abound when we help the suffering or suffer patiently ourselves. Loving Jesus means learning to suffer with him, "...And this is God's doing. For he has graciously granted you the privilege not only of believing in Christ, but of suffering for him as well" (Philippians 1:28-29).

Christian suffering has a purpose. From the beginning of his ministry, Jesus warned, "A disciple is not above the teacher, nor the slave above the master; it is enough for the disciple to be like the teacher, and the slave like the master. If they have called the master of the house Beelzebub, how much more will they malign those of his household" (Matthew 10:24-25). Christians must embrace suffering, as Jesus did, to accomplish the purpose Jesus entrusted to us—to share the good news of the kingdom of God, and there is much work to be done.

Paul suffered to proclaim the Gospel to the Gentiles. After his conversion, Paul could not stop teaching the Truth about Jesus and salvation to everyone. He persisted in the work Jesus gave him no matter the inconvenience, opposition, or danger that awaited him in his travels. He suffered because Jews hated him and Christians were afraid of him. He endured physical infirmity. "Three times I appealed to the Lord about this, that it would leave me, but he said to me, 'My grace is sufficient for you, for power is made perfect in weakness.' So, I will boast all the more gladly of my weaknesses, so that the power of Christ may dwell in me" (2 Corinthians 12:8-9). Paul suffered while he defended his reputation and credentials as an apostle. Paul wrote letters to the Christian Churches, his spiritual children, to encourage them and keep them from being led away from the Gospel, even as he was imprisoned in Rome. Paul escaped many attempts by his rivals to kill him.[63] Paul's sufferings produced good fruit. It is the same for every Christian who chooses to do God's Will. We choose to suffer with Jesus; we choose to love Jesus.

Suffering is different for each person. The suffering of losing a loved one is different for a person with deep faith than for a person with weak faith. Perception and background influence the way a person suffers. Tom and Joe are an example of how two different people suffer the same loss.

Tom and Joe both lose their jobs, investments, and financial security when the company they work for goes bankrupt. They find that their options to recover their losses are limited and will require costly lawsuits. Tom chooses anger. He contemplates revenge day and night and becomes bitter. His anger increases his suffering and darkens his soul. He refuses to cooperate with Joe to pursue legitimate avenues because his trust is shaken. Joe chooses legitimate avenues to resolve the betrayal, and relies on guidance from the Holy Spirit in prayer. Joe suffers with Jesus and, in doing God's Will, becomes an example to others of how to follow Christ. He knows the peace of Christ. Neither individual may see justice in their lifetimes, but the consequences of their choices remains in their souls.

Some people do not believe that Jesus understands what they are going through. He does because he suffered. A woman in labor has already suffered discomfort and anxieties for nine months. She bears her child, a new citizen for the Kingdom of God, which Jesus established when he gave birth to his Church through his Crucifixion and Resurrection. Through the gift of motherhood, she suffers and rejoices with Jesus.

Parents who suffer with Jesus when they see their children falling away from the Gospel, take heart! He knows and loves your children better than you can. Persevere in prayer and good example. Suffering with Jesus will bear fruit. Everyone who suffers the illness or death of a loved one, take heart! "Blessed are those who mourn, for they will be comforted" (Matthew 5:4). You have God's promise. Put aside anger and despair. Be open to receive God's comfort. Keep the hope of eternal life alive.

Don't be like the child who receives an exquisite gift carefully chosen by his loving parents, but after examining it, casts it aside to play with the box. Suffering exists. We choose whether to accept Jesus' offer to share suffering with us, or not. Suffering forms and perfects us, preparing us for the perfection of heaven. Whoever endures suffering patiently, suffers with Jesus. Suffering with Jesus for the salvation of souls is one of the highest forms of evangelization, and a great sign of a soul's degree of love for God and neighbor.

CHAPTER 11

The Cross is the Sum of All Wisdom and Knowledge

· ·

"So the Jews gathered around him and said to him, 'How long will you keep us in suspense? If you are the Messiah, tell us plainly.' Jesus answered, 'I have told you, and you do not believe. The works that I do in my Father's name testify to me; but you do not believe, because you do not belong to my sheep. My sheep hear my voice. I know them, and they follow me. I give them eternal life, and they will never perish. No one will snatch them out of my hand. What my Father has given me is greater than all else, and no one can snatch it out of the Father's hand. The Father and I are one.' The Jews took up stones again to stone him. Jesus replied, 'I have shown you many good works from the Father. For which of these are you going to stone me?'" (John 10:24-32).

The Cross Exposes "the Inner Thoughts of Many"

[64] Many Jews listened to Jesus' teaching, witnessed the miracles he performed, and believed in him. "So the chief priests and the Pharisees called a meeting of the council, and said, 'What are we to do? This man is performing many signs. If we let him go on like this, everyone will believe in him, and the Romans will come and destroy our holy place and our nation.'

But one of them, Caiaphas, who was high priest that year, said to them, 'You know nothing at all! You do not understand that it is better for you to have one man die for the people than to have the whole nation destroyed'" (John 11:47-50).

The Jewish leaders were determined that the people not be allowed to listen to Jesus. They began a program of disinformation to confuse the truth. They plotted to murder Jesus to maintain their power and treasures. If God did not intend for his Messiah to re-establish the kingdom of Israel and save them from Roman oppression, then at least, the leaders thought, they could get the Romans off their backs by eliminating the Messiah. Because of their fear, they sold out Jesus, and, in the process, sold their souls. This is the modus operandi of Satan! They did not trust God's plan so they took matters into their own hands. Consider how the "…inner thoughts of many…" (Luke 2:35) were revealed:

The Lessons Taught by the Cross

Jesus was desolate. After the Last Supper, "They went to a place called Gethsemane; and he said to his disciples, 'Sit here while I pray.' He took with him Peter and James and John, and began to be distressed and agitated. And he said to them, 'I am deeply grieved, even to death; remain here, and keep awake.' And going a little farther, he threw himself on the ground and prayed that, if it were possible, the hour might pass from him. He said, 'Abba, Father, for you all things are possible; remove this cup from me; yet, not what I want, but what you want.'" (Mark 14:32-36). Jesus knew dryness and desolation. His human desires were at odds with God's Will, but he chose obedience. Our Father did not abandon him in his dryness but worked a great miracle through Jesus; Jesus rose from the dead and opened heaven for all humankind. Dryness in the soul happens to almost all who pray, but never be discouraged. Continue in prayer until God reveals his

Will. The Cross teaches us to have courage and not to waiver in saying to our Father, "…yet, not what I want, but what you want…" (Mark 14:36).

Jesus was arrested without cause and quickly and underhandedly placed on trial. The chief priests violated Jewish Law and trumped up charges backed by lying witnesses to condemn him. The Jewish people who admired Jesus had no time to protest the evil plan of their leaders.

Life is not fair. Who knew this better than Jesus did? Even though Jesus was aware of the enemies he faced in Jerusalem, he did not try to escape them. Walking into the temple and facing powerful men bent on murder took courage, but Jesus was on a mission of love. Many souls had not heard about the Kingdom of God. There was much to be done and Jesus greatest act of love was yet to come. The Cross teaches that love requires us to do God's Will courageously with single-mindedness of purpose.

Jesus was accused of blasphemy. Jesus was silent. He did not shrink from his accusers nor did he make excuses to get out of a bad situation. He let the Truth speak. The testimony was there for all to see. Did his accusers not remember the horrifying story that spread through the land about thirty-three years ago? King Herod ordered his troops to kill all the babies less than two years old who lived around Bethlehem because he learned that the Messiah had been born there. Where was the Messiah? What about the man named Jesus who walked around the countryside healing the sick and casting out demons? He was about the right age. Everyone wanted to see him and be healed or have a loved one healed. Jesus even raised the dead! There was the little girl, and the son of the widowed mother, and Lazarus, a good man with many friends, who was raised to life by Jesus in a town just outside of Jerusalem after he had been dead four days! Who but God could do these things?! Yet Jesus was accused of blasphemy.

Who among us has not been falsely accused? It is part of our common human story, ranking with death and taxes. Even little ones will falsely accuse playmates if they believe they are about to get into trouble. We do not seem to outgrow lying! It is a never ending human dilemma: How can we stop!? James said, "But if you have bitter envy and selfish ambition in your hearts, do not be boastful and false to the truth. Such wisdom does not come down from above, but is earthly, unspiritual, devilish. For where there is envy and selfish ambition, there will also be disorder and wickedness of every kind. But the wisdom from above is first pure, then peaceable, gentle, willing to yield, full of mercy and good fruits, without trace of partiality or hypocrisy" (James 3:14-17). The Cross teaches us how to live "the wisdom from above."

Jesus was scourged. Jesus was pure, holy, and perfect. He never sinned. Evil hates what is pure, holy, and perfect. Satan can't get a foothold! Where are the vices to exploit? Jesus forgave his enemies. The devil hates people who refuse to hate. Where is sin of wrath?! But pure hearts love their enemies and pray for them. They recognize that their enemies face eternal consequences for their sins and feel the sadness of Jesus at their loss.

What about vices like greed, lust, gluttony, and jealousy? The Evil One cannot fathom a human soul without them! But pure hearts focus on loving God. God is the total object of their desire and he fills them with grace. Evil believes that, surely, every human soul must give in to sinful pride. No! Not the pure in heart, for they have given themselves to God in complete humility. God, in return, honors them and shares his life with them. To the pure in heart, human pride is like dust in the wind.

Evil often relies on his old standby, sloth. In the end, souls regret mostly the good deeds not done. Evil can easily mix up a temptation concoction: start with a cup of self-doubt, add a cup of second-guessing, and a dash of natural laziness, and voila! Sloth! But the pure in heart are tuned into God's Will. They focus on his plan with single-minded purpose. They find no pleasure in neglecting God's work. It gives them joy.

Purity in the human heart causes great confusion to Evil. Jesus said, "Blessed are the pure in heart, for they will see God" (Matthew 5:8). A pure heart is attainable, for Jesus does not send us on senseless quests. He showed us how. Jesus chose love and obedience to our Father over personal comfort, and patiently endured the resulting suffering. The Cross teaches us the way to a pure heart is to practice self-sacrificing love, no matter the cost.

Jesus was crowned with thorns. When Pilate asked Jesus if he were a king, "Jesus answered, 'My kingdom is not from this world. If my kingdom were from this world, my followers would be fighting to keep me from being handed over to the Jews. But as it is, my kingdom is not from here.' Pilate asked him, 'So you are a king?' Jesus answered, 'You say that I am a king. For this I was born, and for this I came into the world, to testify to the truth. Everyone who belongs to the truth listens to my voice'" (John 18:36-37). Jesus is a king and we are citizens of his Kingdom if we listen to his voice. Paul taught, "He (God)[65] has rescued us from the power of darkness and transferred us into the kingdom of his beloved Son, in whom we have redemption, the forgiveness of sins" (Colossians 1:13-14). But, like Jesus, our "kingdom is not of this world." Obstacles, caused by temptations from the devil, the flesh, and the world, threaten to cost us our place in the Kingdom. It is easy to place our faith in the power and honors of this world instead of the next. Remember, Jesus was honored in this world by a plaque inscribed, "Jesus of Nazareth, the King of the Jews,"[66] nailed to the cross above his head.

Strive to say with Paul, "Yet whatever gains I had, these I have come to regard as loss because of Christ. More than that, I regard everything as loss because of the surpassing value of knowing Christ Jesus my Lord... (Philippians 3:7-8). The Cross teaches us to have faith in our Lord, to trust him, and to follow him with undivided loyalty.

Jesus was stripped and nailed to a cross to die the death reserved for criminals. He was left to hang naked for all to see, onlookers jeering at him. His enemies thought his degrading and shameful death would put an end to Jesus' cult and dishearten his followers. It did–for three days. When Jesus appeared in the room where the disciples were staying, his first words to them were, "…Peace be with you" (Luke 24:36). Jesus was alive! The horror was over. The disciples' faith, that had been terribly shaken, was renewed. Strengthened by the Holy Spirit, they would soon risk all for the kingdom of God. The Cross teaches us that if we remain firm in our faith, nothing will overwhelm us. We have victory in the Cross.

Jesus' heart was pierced through by a sword. This final mockery was an attack on the very nature of God. God is love. By piercing Jesus' heart, Evil tried to destroy the heart of love incarnate. "…one of the soldiers pierced his side with a spear, and at once blood and water came out" (John 19:34). Blood and water poured out as proof of God's enduring love and mercy. Eternal life was opened to us. By the Cross, we are set free!

The Cross is our salvation. It most perfectly represents Christianity. It is the sign chosen by God himself, suffering leading to perfection. "It is fitting that God, for whom and through whom all things exist, in bringing many children to glory, should make the pioneer of their salvation (Jesus)[67] perfect through sufferings" (Hebrews 2:10). Suffering exists. We find ourselves in devastating situations through no fault of our own. We invite suffering by our own actions because we lack understanding of their consequences. We suffer illnesses, injury, and loss of loved ones. We suffer from heat, cold, hunger and thirst. We suffer exposure to our unstable environment: hurricanes, tornados, flooding, earthquakes, illness, etc. This is not how God wanted us to live. God intended for us to live in union with him, enjoying his gifts, but due to humankind's ongoing rejection of God's sovereignty, this is the world we have. But even now, God strengthens, and gives guidance and comfort to those who willingly accept their sufferings, their crosses, while obeying God's Will. The Cross reminds us of how Jesus coped with this world and is the example that we are to follow, always remembering that, after the suffering of this short life, we can go home to the place Jesus prepared for us in the Kingdom of Heaven.

***

"The steadfast love of the Lord never ceases,

his mercies never come to an end;

they are new every morning; great is your faithfulness.

'The Lord is my portion,' says my soul, 'therefore I will hope in him.'

The Lord is good to those who wait for him, to the soul that seeks him.

It is good that one should wait quietly for the salvation of the Lord.

It is good for one to bear the yoke in youth,

to sit alone in silence when the Lord has imposed it,

to put one's mouth to the dust (there may yet be hope),

to give one's cheek to the smiter, and be filled with insults.

For the Lord will not reject forever.

Although he causes grief,

he will have compassion according to the abundance of his steadfast love;

for he does not willingly afflict or grieve anyone."

The Book of Lamentations 3:22-33

***

CHAPTER 12

Journey to Union

....

"They who have my commandments and keep them are those who love me; and those who love me will be loved by my Father, and I will love them and reveal myself to them" (John 14:21). This revelation is union with God. Union is the grace God gives to loving, obedient souls who offer themselves entirely to God in purity of heart to answer God's invitation to enjoy "...every spiritual blessing in the heavenly places" (Ephesians 1:3). "Blessed be the God and Father of our Lord Jesus Christ, who has blessed us in Christ with every spiritual blessing in the heavenly places, just as he chose us in Christ before the foundation of the world to be holy and blameless before him in love. He destined us for adoption as his children through Jesus Christ, according to the good pleasure of his will, to the praise of his glorious grace that he freely bestowed on us in the Beloved" (Ephesians 1:3-7).

God gives his children spiritual joy and encouragement while they dwell in this world. Union with God in pure profound love is our inheritance, and God gives a taste of our inheritance to some while they still dwell in this world. These souls conform to God's Will most perfectly and draw wisdom, strength, and insight from their close relationship with God. Jesus links this purest love to obedience; obedience, which is not a burden, but pure freedom, light and joy.

Our journey to union begins at conception when God gives us a human soul. Our souls are prepared when we are anointed priests, prophets, and kings at baptism. Jesus makes it clear that we are created for union with God with his command: "Abide in me as I abide in you. Just as the branch cannot bear fruit by itself unless it abides in the vine, neither can you unless you abide in me. I am the vine, you are the branches. Those who abide in me and I in them bear much fruit, because apart from me you can do nothing" (John 15:4-5). Our purpose in life is union with God because separated from him we "can do nothing." Then Jesus warns, "Whoever does not abide in me is thrown away like a branch and withers; such branches are gathered, thrown into the fire, and burned" (John 15:6). If a soul walks away from Jesus, it cuts itself off from the source of life and good things. A soul separated from Christ must repent and be reconnected to the vine or it risks allying itself with Satan and being "…thrown into the fire and burned." We are not speaking here of souls who have had no opportunity to know Jesus, but souls who reject him. And Jesus promises, "If you abide in me, and my words abide in you, ask for whatever you wish, and it will be done for you" (John 15:7). Souls who abide in Jesus would not dream of asking for something that is not in conformity with God's Will. Just the thought would trouble them deeply.

God made us to share happiness with him. We are not puppets or slaves of God, but children, "and if children, then heirs, heirs of God and joint heirs with Christ—if, in fact, we suffer with him so that we may also be glorified with him" (Romans 8:17). The only thing God asks of us is the loyalty that children owe their parents. "Suffering with him" means accepting as Jesus did the hardships we encounter as we choose to live his Will, so that we may share his glory and eternal happiness. As we grow closer to God, we are invited to share our wisdom and joy with others.

Our Prophetic Calling

Spreading the Word of God requires our cooperation. It's time to revisit our friend Pat.

One morning, Pat sat at the kitchen table with a cup of coffee and the Bible:

Jesus: "Good Morning, Pat."

Pat: "Lord, Jesus! I was just praying for peace. I am glad you are here. Things are a mess down here. It is so frustrating that nothing I do makes any difference."

Jesus: "I heard you, Pat, and thank-you for your prayers and wishes. I appreciate it when you take the time to talk to me. Your prayers *are* making a difference even when humankind has made my creation so complicated that it is difficult to see the answers to your prayers."

Pat: "All of this chaos makes my heart hurt."

Jesus: "I know, Pat, mine, too. I desire to send our Father's graces, but people refuse my help. They believe their wisdom is greater than mine and try to solve the world's problems without me. They refuse the wisdom of the Holy Spirit. They are lost in their false pride and arrogance. The result is the chaos and the confusion of the Evil One. If they do not follow me, then they follow the Evil One. I grieve for souls who choose not to know me. The Evil One deceives them into thinking that they can do good apart from me. That is the greatest lie."

Pat: "I've never seen you so sad before. Can I help? What can I do to help?"

Jesus: "You have a loving and generous heart, Pat. There is something you can do. Be my hands and my feet and my voice among my children."

Pat: "What do I have to do?"

Jesus: "You do not 'have to' do anything, Pat. I am asking you."

Pat: "What are you asking me to do?"

Jesus: "I have taught you many things about the Kingdom of God in your prayers and reading. I would like you to tell others about me. Tell them I love them, but I can no longer be patient. The blood of my murdered little ones cries out to me for justice as did the blood of my servant, Abel. I hear the prayers of my suffering children who cry out for justice. Remember my prophets? Like them, tell my children to repent and stop their evil practices. Tell them to stop rejecting me and our Father's graces. Tell my children to follow me and serve me just as I served our Father. Tell them if they refuse me, they are refusing the place I have prepared for them in heaven. Tell my children to make time for me, to pray, and I will guide them. Tell them I am waiting for them. Tell them life is short."

Pat: "That is a lot to do. Where do I start?"

Jesus: "I will guide you. Speak to your family and friends."

Pat: "It will be hard. At work, I can get in trouble for talking about you. My co-workers will be afraid of being fired! People are getting in trouble because they actively practice Christianity. And some of my friends won't put their phones down long enough to listen! I guess I could text them. Some people will think I am joking. I could not stand people being disrespectful to you, but they...."

Jesus: "Pat, be at peace. I appreciate your honest appraisal of the situation. I know the world into which I am sending you. Don't you remember what I told my disciples? I will give you the words at the proper moment. Trust me. Some people will listen and rejoice with you in my Word. Others will not listen. Think of your work as planting a seed in them. I will send others to water it."

Pat: "I guess that with you, I can do anything."

Jesus: "Don't guess! Know that with me, you can do anything. Did I not help Moses part the sea?"

Pat: "That would make news! Can I have a staff, too?"

Jesus, laughing: "I enjoy our conversations, Pat. If any seas need parting, I will provide the staff. So, will you help my children?"

Pat: "Please show me how and when to talk, and please don't leave me alone."

Jesus: "Thank-you, Pat, you are never alone. I am always with you. That is my promise."

We all receive a prophetic calling similar to Pat's. If we say yes, we receive the graces needed to answer God's call. People do not usually hear God's call with their ears. The great grace our friend Pat received must be accompanied by an equally great grace of discernment and spiritual guidance, so it could be determined whether the words came from Jesus, the human imagination, or the devil.

God calls Christians to be his prophets. Sometimes, we hear his call in the voices of our families, friends, mentors, or complete strangers. Sometimes, we discover a talent and enjoy putting it to use to help others. We are happy when we use the gifts God gives us to do his Will. That is one way God guides us. We might read an article or book that speaks directly to our souls. Often, our intellect analyzes our actions and situation and, based upon our knowledge of God's Law, we logically choose his Will.

God speaks to each of us personally and in unique ways, just as he made each one of us a unique stone to be fitted into his holy temple. Refusing God's Will leaves a gap in the temple walls, a unique gift that is not shared, an empty space that weakens faith and charity. When Christians succumb to corrupt propaganda and refuse God's Will, it is a serious matter. Charity grows weak. The Church drifts away from the apostolic truths as careless Christians compromise the integrity of their faith. Increasing numbers of people disregard our Father's commandments, calling them unenlightened, and make up 'enlightened' rules they think should be OK with God. They make themselves gods.

God's commandments are light! Souls, who deny God's Will, become lost in darkness and cause suffering, chaos, and confusion in our world. It is foolishness to refuse God's call. God's call is a great gift that answers the age-old question, "What is the purpose of my life? Why am I here?" To learn God's Will, meditate upon what makes your soul happy. Your soul is eternal; this body will die. Focus on Jesus and enjoy his presence in your soul. Take the time to be quiet in prayer.

Biblical Prophecy Fulfilled

Prophecy is from the Holy Spirit and everything from God comes to fulfillment. For example:

God said to Abraham, "… 'Look toward heaven and count the stars, if you are able to count them.' Then he said to him, 'So shall your descendants be.'" (Genesis 15:5). Centuries later, King Solomon, the son of David, asked God for wisdom to govern his people, saying, "And your servant is in the midst of the people whom you have chosen, a great people, so numerous they cannot be numbered or counted" (1 Kings 3:8). Add to the innumerable Israelites the equally innumerable descendants of Ishmael, Abraham's elder son. Prophecy fulfilled.

And, "Then Moses went up from the plains of Moab to Mount Nebo, to the top of Pisgah, which is opposite Jericho, and the Lord showed him the whole land: Gilead as far as Dan, all Naphtali, the land of Ephraim and Manasseh, all the land of Judah as far as the Western Sea, the Negeb, and the Plain—that is, the valley of Jericho, the city of palm trees—as far as

Zoar. The Lord said to him, 'This is the land of which I swore to Abraham, to Isaac, and to Jacob, saying, 'I will give it to your descendants...'" (Deuteronomy 34:1-4). Moses died and Joshua was chosen as his successor. He led the Israelite people to victory after victory by the hand of God as they conquered the Promised Land. "So Joshua took the whole land, according to all that the Lord had spoken to Moses; and Joshua gave it for an inheritance to Israel according to their tribal allotments. And the land had rest from war" (Joshua 11:23). Prophecy fulfilled.

And, "Now the word of the Lord came to Jonah son of Amittai, saying, 'Go at once to Ninevah, that great city, and cry out against it; for their wickedness has come up before me.'" (Jonah 1:1-2). "Jonah began to go into the city, going a day's walk. And he cried out, 'Forty days more, and Ninevah shall be overthrown!' And the people of Ninevah believed God; they proclaimed a fast, and everyone, great and small, put on sackcloth" (Jonah 3:4-5). "When God saw what they did, how they turned from their evil ways, God changed his mind about the calamity that he had said he would bring upon them; and he did not do it" (Jonah 3:10). God wanted the people of Ninevah to stop their wickedness. Jonah's prophetic mission had the best possible outcome; the people repented and turned back to God. The prophecy was fulfilled, but Jonah did not see it that way. He was looking forward to the destruction of Ninevah, but instead, God revealed the depths of his mercy through Jonah. Jonah had a temper tantrum. Read God's justification for his actions in Jonah 4:1-11. Prophecy filled.

And, remember Jeremiah? Zedekiah, King of Judah, was facing a serious decision. Judah was about to be overrun by the forces of King Nebuchadrezzar of Babylon. Little Judah occupied a bit of ground between the great powers of Egypt and Babylon and King Zedekiah chose to ally Judah with Egypt pitting Egypt against Babylon for control of Judah. This displeased God who had already rescued Judah from Egypt once through Moses and did not want to do it again. Jeremiah was one prophet among many in Judah. False prophets spoke lies to please the King and thus benefitted from the King's favor. Jeremiah spoke God's Word and that did not please the King. Jeremiah was arrested, imprisoned, tossed in a well, and left to die. Still, he prophesied the truth. But, King Zedekiah doubted the counsel of the false prophets so he secretly contacted Jeremiah who, speaking the word of God, advised him to surrender Judah to Babylon. Jeremiah gave Zedekiah God's promise that King Nebuchadrezzar would be merciful and he would be safe. Not surrendering meant that the Jerusalem would be destroyed. King Zedekiah refused to surrender fearing his personal safety. Jerusalem was not rescued by Egypt as Zedekiah had planned, but was overrun and burned to the ground. Zedekiah's sons were killed and Zedekiah was blinded. (See Jeremiah: 38, 39 and 52). Prophecy fulfilled.

And, "As he came out of the temple, one of his disciples said to him, 'Look, Teacher, what large stones and what large buildings!' Then Jesus asked him, 'Do you see these great buildings? Not one stone will be left here upon another; all will be thrown down.'" (Mark 13:1-2). The temple was completely destroyed in 70 AD by the Romans. Prophecy fulfilled

Biblical Prophecy Yet to Be Fulfilled

After Jesus prophesied the destruction of the temple, "When he was sitting on the Mount of Olives, the disciples came to him privately, saying, 'Tell us, when this will be, and what will be the sign of your coming and of the end of the age?'" (Matthew 24:3).

Jesus answered them, "Beware that no one leads you astray. For many will come in my name, saying, 'I am the Messiah!' and they will lead many astray" (Matthew 24:4-5).

Many have been led astray by heretics: the Arians, the Nestorians, the Gnostics, and all those who deny inconvenient parts of the Truth Jesus taught. More recently: In the United States, Jim Jones, a community organizer, founded the People's Temple as a Christian community church. A self-proclaimed messiah, Jones turned away from Christianity and led his hopeless flock to mass suicide at Jonestown, Guyana in November of 1978 (Jim Jones). In 1993, David Koresh led a Christian sect called the Branch Davidians. A self-proclaimed prophet, he believed he would father the Chosen One. He led seventy-six members of his community to fiery deaths when child abuse and weapons charges prompted the United States Attorney General to end to a fifty-one-day siege of his Waco, Texas, Mount Carmel Center compound (David Koresh). Shoko Asahara founded Aum Shinrikyo, a nominally Christian sect, in Japan. Another self-proclaimed messiah, he inspired his flock to release sarin nerve gas into the Tokyo subway system in 1995, killing thirteen people (Shoko Asahara). These are just a few. False messiahs, heretics, use cults of personality, claims of unique mission and "better" doctrine, and devious rhetoric to lure people to their "religions." They create confusion that results in the loss of the peace of Christ. What grief and chaos they cause!

Jesus' warning not to be led astray is very timely. After warning his disciples, Jesus told them:

"And you will hear of wars and rumors of wars; see that you are not alarmed; for this must take place, but the end is not yet. For nation will rise against nation, and kingdom against kingdom, and there will be famines and earthquakes in various places: all this is but the beginning of the birth pangs" (Matthew 24:6-8).

Wars and famine are caused by sins against charity. Paul explains the reason for natural disaster: "We know that the whole creation has been groaning in labor pains until now; and not only the creation, but we ourselves, who have the first fruits of the Spirit, groan inwardly while we wait for adoption, the redemption of our bodies" (Romans 8:22-23). All of creation became disordered when Adam and Eve lost paradise. All of creation will be restored at the end of the ages when Jesus returns as the Just Judge.

Then the righteous will receive glorified bodies, creation will be put back in order, and Paradise will be restored. What are Christians to do until then? Follow the lead of Jesus and help the suffering. Christians are the active love of Christ in the world. Wars, earthquakes, and famine will happen, but they are, "the beginning of the birth pangs,"[68] the birth of "a new heaven and a new earth" promised[69]to those who love God.

Jesus continued, "Then they will hand you over to be tortured and will put you to death, and you will be hated by all nations because of my name. Then many will fall away, and they will betray one another and hate one another. (Matthew 24:9-10).

There is an historical perspective to this prophecy. Roman governors and emperors viciously persecuted Christians off and on, until Christianity was made legal. For centuries, the Christian Church grew, until the Protestant Revolution set off a wave of the worst kind of persecution, Christian against Christian: Catholic against Protestant, Protestant against Protestant, and Catholic against Catholic. The violence was horrifying as Christianity began its division into thousands of sects. In England, for example, King Henry VIII, in need of a male heir, divorced his wife and married Anne Boleyn. The Pope excommunicated him, so he set himself up as head of a new church, the Church of England. Henry VIII had the Roman Catholic Church banished in England, killed many priests, and closed churches and monasteries and seized the property for England. Henry executed Sir Thomas More, his loyal advisor, and many others because they would not reject Catholicism and pledge allegiance to the Church of England. Protestants in France were persecuted until the French Revolution when the National Assembly granted the freedom to practice one's religion. But the French Revolution resulted in the seizure of Catholic church property, monasteries, and convents to help pay the French national debt, as well as, the execution of many priests, who refused to violate their priestly vows by pledging allegiance to the new French government. Entire convents of nuns also were murdered.

In the seventeenth century, small Protestant sects fled to America looking for freedom from mainstream Protestant tyranny. They established colonies and advanced the concept of religious freedom. Ironically, in most of the colonies, Catholic Christians were prevented by laws from holding religious services and public office. Only the colony of Maryland allowed Catholic Christians what Americans now consider basic civil rights.

Christianity honors the choice inherent in free will. Jesus offers the opportunity to choose him. Sadly, there are few places in the world where Christianity truly enjoys freedom. Persecution often takes the subtle form of intimidating and ostracizing Christians who live their faith. It can begin as a slight change in the political rhetoric from "freedom of religion" to "freedom of worship." (Hitler allowed "freedom of worship," but only his Nazi sanctioned-version of religion. He did not allow "freedom of religion.") Or, it can begin as violently as genocide by jihadists.

Monsignor Charles Pope, from the Archdiocese of Washington, D.C., in his blog, lists five stages of persecution as generally recognized by sociologists: stereotyping, vilifying, marginalizing, criminalizing and outright persecution (Craine). Reviewing these stages reveals an anti-Christian bias creeping into an increasingly materialistic and atheistic common thinking. The consequential changes in societal attitudes re-form the norm and the norm is becoming decidedly un-Christian.

Christians are stereotyped as narrow-minded bigots or superstitious fools because they defend God's Truth. They have the wisdom to recognize sin, and so, are vilified as agitators and religious zealots when they oppose the "right" to abortion and other public sponsorship of sin. The simple logic of Truth rouses consciences and makes people uncomfortable, especially in countries which advance moral relativism (that is, each person decides what is "right" for him/herself), or extremism (mercy is excluded). People hate the pain of their consciences telling them they are wrong, so they practice all kinds of perverted thinking, even to the extreme of blaming psychiatric disease or genetic pre-disposition or bad parents or even Christian teaching as the cause of their bad consciences. Their logic is "If Christians weren't telling me it is a sin, then I wouldn't feel so bad about doing it." Instead of searching for the Truth to ease their consciences, they falsely justify their sins and shoot the messenger. They vilify Christians.

Vilification leads to marginalization. Christians are marginalized because the Truth they cling to does not conform to new societal norms. They believe in Christ. They practice virtue and their light cannot be hidden. They are marginalized as foolish for their steadfast faith in God and everlasting life. Christians are stripped of their holy days, once honored around the world. Christmas and Easter are mocked as generic holidays and Jesus' example of generous sacrifice is replaced by greed. Children receive their Christmas presents and Easter baskets but do not know Jesus, the originator of the feasts. Christ is the only true source of love. Those who mock Jesus are without love. They use their "feel good" and "politically correct" morality to marginalize Christ's followers.

It is easy to criminalize the marginalized. The marginalized have no power. Are Christians being criminalized? You decide. In 2013, husband and wife bakery owners in Oregon, U.S.A. refused to make a wedding cake for a same-sex couple because doing so violated their consciences. The same-sex couple filed a complaint with the State of Oregon, which ruled that the bakery owners had violated their civil rights. Oregon threatened outrageous fines for "civil rights violations" if the bakers refuse to be "rehabilitated." The little bakery owners courageously refused to violate their consciences. They face economic and social martyrdom (Harkness). After a courageous fight, they lost their business. Adults at a Senior Center in Georgia, U.S.A. were told they could no longer say grace before they ate their U.S. Federal Government-funded lunch. Only a "moment of silence" was permitted. After the community pushed back, the new Department of Human Services head of Aging Services "clarified" the agency's position, and the non-profit that administered the lunch program was able to allow prayer before lunch (Montoya). U.S. Courts ban the public display of crosses, public prayer, and Christmas crèches. The Ten Commandments are not permitted to be displayed in courtrooms. What insanity! Government cuts the legs off the ladder upon which it stands! Without the guidance of the Ten Commandments, justice is whatever the powerful decide, without limitation! They have uncontrolled power over citizens without the morality inherent in the Ten Commandments! Christians who will not take part in paying government-mandated abortion taxes and insurance premiums are criminalized. Canadian law criminalizes the use of Bible verses to publicly defend the Christian position against same-sex marriage! Bible verses are called hate speech instead of Truth. These few examples are the tip of the iceberg. Around the world, Christians' movements are limited, they are excessively taxed, and they are imprisoned for being Christian. Is Christian criminalization coming to a town near you?

Wishy-washy Christians think they are free of responsibility for public sin. They are not! They cover their eyes and say to God, "You can't see me," like silly children. Every Christian must stand up against evil! To hide one's eyes is to endorse the sin. ***Christians have power to change evil when they stand together in the truth and in prayer.*** There is no time left. Even some Christian religions have bowed to political pressure to accept and even participate in sinful practices, betraying the Truth they have held for centuries.

Persecution of Christians in Western countries by atheists, communists, and other God-rejecters is sneaky and insidious. The intention is to neutralize unwavering Christians so that only misled and wishy-washy followers will be left to wield civil power. As outright Christian persecution gains acceptance in Western culture, the persecutors include the misled and the wishy-washy. Even now, Satan mocks God through self-proclaimed Christian civil leaders, who impose corrupt laws and onerous regulations upon those who live the Gospel. The sad result is confusion among people who follow so-called Christian civil leaders expecting them to be good examples of Christianity. Confusion is Satan's weapon.

Some governments allow only government-sanctioned religions, code words meaning they want Christians to compromise the Truth. Not compromising has resulted in Christians being driven out of the places where Christianity was founded and established, from its ancient roots. Christians are "tortured and put to death." In 2014, Chaldean Christians were murdered or driven out of Mosul, Iraq by Islamic jihadists. The Christians who fled were terrorized and robbed of their belongings at checkpoints and an eighteen-hundred-year-old Chaldean Catholic Church was burned by the jihadists (Blair). Christians are being coerced to make them do what true followers of Christ cannot do—compromise their faith. In communist countries, Christianity cannot be freely practiced. Pastors are imprisoned and Christian communities must worship in secret places to avoid arrest. "... Here is a call for the endurance and faith of the saints" (Revelations 13:10).

"And because of the increase of lawlessness, the love of many will grow cold. But the one who endures to the end will be saved" (Matthew 24:12-13).

"Lawlessness" is sin. Every sin is a crime against love. Foolish people sin repeatedly without remorse until the resulting misery becomes "normal." The more that sin is accepted as normal, the more normal lawlessness becomes. Even common courtesies, which are little acts of love, are forgotten. The psalmist wrote, "for look, the wicked bend the bow, they have fitted their arrow to the string, to shoot in the dark at the upright in heart. If the foundations are destroyed, what can the righteous do" (Psalm 11:2-3).

In the end, evil will seem virtuous and many will be confused. "But you, beloved, must remember the predictions of the apostles of our Lord Jesus Christ; for they said to you, 'In the last time there will be scoffers, indulging in their own ungodly lusts.' It is these worldly people, devoid of the Spirit, who are causing divisions. But you, beloved, build yourselves up on your most holy faith; pray in the Holy Spirit; keep yourselves in the love of God; look forward to the mercy of our Lord Jesus Christ that leads to eternal life. And have mercy on some who are wavering; save others by snatching them out of the fire; have mercy on still others with fear, hating even the tunics defiled by their bodies" (Jude 17-23).

Love God and neighbor, pray in the Holy Spirit, avoid sin, ask for Christ's mercy for everyone, even for the worst of sinners, and be strong in the Faith. In light of Jude's advice, how can Christians justify their sectarian bickering? If Christians will not be Christ to each other, how can they effectively be the love and mercy of Christ in a world that does not know him? Christians must adhere to the Truth taught by Jesus Christ, but the sad fact is that Christianity is under attack by ignorant Christians! Sectarian bickering causes the love of many to grow cold. How does it look to the God-seeker when one Christian professes one thing while another Christian claims the opposite! What has the God-seeker learned but disrespect for Christians? Corruption of Christ's message is defeating his Church.

How confused Christians have become! Christ's followers are required to live love and obedience! Obedience will bring the Christian branches into unity with Jesus, the vine, and unite all Christians. Obedience to love and God's commandments will heal Christ's Church.

"And this good news of the kingdom will be proclaimed throughout the world, as testimony to all the nations..." (Matthew 24:14).

There has been much scholarly debate about what "throughout the world" and "all the nations" means. Does it mean every person will hear about Jesus or just some people in every nation? Will mass media do the trick? God is loving and merciful beyond our understanding. We will leave the fulfillment of this passage to his mercy.

"...and then the end will come" (Matthew 24:14).

The End of the Ages

What will happen at the end? Heaven or hell, it is your choice. There is no middle ground. Each person is like a child holding a basket waiting for gifts. When the gifts come, some children keep the ones they like and toss away the gifts they do not want, some children refuse to open their baskets to receive the gifts, and some receive the gifts gratefully. The baskets are our souls; the gifts are graces from God. The children, who gratefully accept God's graces, even when they are difficult or painful, are the ones who love God. They have eternal life. The children who accept only the gifts they like are the lukewarm. Of them Jesus says, "So, because you are lukewarm, and neither cold nor hot, I am about to spit you out of my mouth" (Revelations 3:16). They are in danger of choosing hell by default, and they know it. The children who refuse to open their baskets have already chosen Satan.

"If you invoke as Father the one who judges all people impartially according to their deeds, live in reverent fear during the time of your exile. You know that you were ransomed from the futile ways inherited from your ancestors, not with perishable things like silver or gold, but with the precious blood of Christ, like that of a lamb without defect or blemish. He was destined before the foundation of the world, but was revealed at the end of the ages for your sake. Through him you have come to trust in God, who raised him from the dead and gave him glory, so that your faith and hope are set on God" (1 Peter 1:17-21).

The "end of the ages" began with Christ's conception in the womb of Mary. It continues to this day and will continue until Christ comes to judge all humankind. Peter encourages us to live in "reverent fear" of God. We have no power of our own. We cannot control the weather, or death, or the consequences of our decisions. We have nothing but our faith in God's mercy, our hope for eternal life, our love for him, and our certainty of his love for us. We live in fear of our weakness. We fear losing God; we fear God's judgment. However, fear of the Lord is not like the terror felt when one is in imminent danger, but a profound awe at the goodness of God, a deeply held respect for his power and justice, faith and trust in the perfection of his judgments, and delight at the tenderness of his love. So, with that understanding of the gift of 'reverent fear,' and gratefully acknowledging the gift of eternal life purchased by the slaughter of the Lamb of God, we can address "the end."

CHAPTER 13

Blessed Are Those Who Follow the Lamb

In the last book of the Bible, Revelation, John shares the spiritual visions and knowledge he received while he was exiled on the Island of Patmos for proclaiming Christ. In the first century A.D., Christians needed encouragement. Christians of Jewish background were thrown out of synagogues and branded as traitors by their families and friends. Some, like Stephen, were martyred. Many Christians fled Jerusalem and settled among the Gentiles. Then, in 64 A.D., Roman Emperor Nero blamed Christians for a great fire in Rome and a more vicious persecution began. Christians who refused to make sacrifices to pagan gods were called heretics and brutally murdered but, by the grace of God, Christianity survived. In the midst of this suffering, John received a revelation from Christ assuring him of the Church's ultimate victory.

Revelation is prophecy primarily concerned with eternal salvation and Christ is the central player. John describes Christ as "…him who is and who was and who is to come…" (Revelation 1:4). "…the faithful witness, the firstborn of the dead, and ruler of the kings of the earth…" (Revelation 1:5). "…the Alpha and the Omega…" (Revelation 1:8), and "… one like the Son of Man, clothed with a long robe and with a golden sash across his chest. His head and his hair were white as white wool, white as snow; his eyes were like a flame of fire, his feet were like burnished bronze, refined as in a furnace, and his voice was like the sound of many waters. In his right hand he held seven stars, and from his mouth came a sharp, two-edged sword, and his face was like the sun shining with full force" (Revelation 1:13-16). These descriptions are difficult to grasp unless they are understood as describing the attributes of our Messiah.

It is obvious to the reader of Revelation that much symbolism is used—beasts and dragons represent Satan, and metaphors of gold and jewels are used to describe heavenly scenes where the indescribably beautiful is translated into images we relate to as desirable. Earthly beauty helps us to long for the infinite grandeur of God and the exquisite beauty of heaven. Some numbers and phrases have symbolic meanings. Just as we say "gazillions" to means an infinite number and "millions" to mean a large, but not uncountable number, John used similar cultural expressions. In Revelation, the number four represents all creation, as in the four corners of the earth. The number seven signifies all, fullness, or completeness, as when Jesus told Peter he must forgive seventy times seven times, meaning always forgive. Six, falling short of seven, represents imperfection. Ten indicates that the referenced occurrence or thing is limited. The fraction ½, (like 3 ½), means that whatever it references will happen for a limited time. One thousand (10x10x10) symbolizes a large but limited number. Twelve represents all the people of the twelve tribes of Israel, or the all of the followers of Jesus' twelve apostles.

The Seven Churches

Jesus instructs John, "Now write what you have seen, what is, and what is to take place after this" (Revelation 1:19). John is told to send the book, which includes detailed messages, to seven churches,[70] specifically the churches at Ephesus, Smyrna, Pergamum, Thyatira, Sardis, Philadelphia, and Laodicea. There were more than seven Christian churches at that time. Paul wrote pastoral letters to churches in Corinth, Galatia, Philippi, and Thessalonica, among others. The number seven indicates that the Book of Revelation, addressed to seven churches, is in truth, addressed to all of Christianity for all time. What does Christ say to the churches?

Ephesus – Jesus praises the Christians at Ephesus for their patient endurance, hard work, and defense of the Faith against heretics; but he warns them, "…you have abandoned the love you had at first. Remember then from what you have fallen; repent, and do the works you did at first. If not, I will come to you and remove your lampstand from its place, unless you repent" (Revelation 2:4-5). Their love is growing cold and they risk losing love, which defines Christianity. But all is not lost. Jesus promises them: "…To everyone who conquers, I will give permission to eat from the tree of life that is in the paradise of God" (Revelation 2:7).

Smyrna – Jesus comforts the Christians at Smyrna, telling them, "I know your affliction and your poverty, even though you are rich…" (Revelation 2:9). They are rich in God's grace and favor. Jesus tells them they will suffer for a limited time, "ten days,"[71] and tells them not to fear these sufferings. There is no warning for the church at Smyrna, only encouragement and the promise: "…Be faithful unto death, and I will give you the crown of life" (Revelation 2:10). And, "… Whoever conquers will not be harmed by the second death" (Revelation 2:11). The "second death"[72] is the sentence passed by Christ at the final judgment of souls who have rejected God.

Pergamum – Jesus praises the community at Pergamum for keeping their faith, in spite of the strong pagan influences around them, even to the point of enduring martyrdom. Some members, however, have failed Christ, fallen into pagan worship practices, and embraced heretical teachings. He warns them: "Repent then. If not, I will come to you soon and make war against them with the sword of my mouth" (Revelation 2:16). Christ defends the purity of his Church. Jesus also encourages them: "…To everyone who conquers I will give some of the hidden manna, and I will give a white stone, and on the white stone is written a new name that no one knows except the one who receives it" (Revelation 2:17). The "hidden manna" is spiritual food. The white stone with the unique name? White is the color of victory; stone is unyielding; and "the new name that no one knows except the one who receives it" reflects God's unique relationship with each soul.

Thyatira– Jesus praises the Christians at Thyatira, "I know your works—your love, faith, service, and patient endurance. I know that your last works are greater than the first" (Revelation 2:19). But they also have a real problem. A "Jezebel,"[73] a woman who calls herself a prophet, is leading some of the community's members into idolatry, (called "adultery" and "fornication"[74] because they are flirting with pagan gods instead of being faithful to Christ). On the Jezebel and her followers, Jesus proclaims judgment: "Beware, I am throwing her on a bed, and those who commit adultery with her I am throwing into great distress, unless they repent of their doings; and I will strike her children dead. And all the churches will know that I am the one who searches minds and hearts, and I will give to each of you as your works deserve" (Revelation 2:22-23). To the faithful ones, Jesus says, "only hold fast to what you have until I come" (Revelation 2:25). Then he promises: "To everyone who conquers and continues to do my works to the end, I will give authority over the nations; to rule them with an iron rod, as when clay pots are shattered—even as I also received authority from my Father. To the one who conquers I will also give the morning star" (Revelation 2:26-28). To those who endure to the end, Jesus gives himself, "…the bright morning star" (Revelation 22:16).

Sardis –The church in Sardis is in serious trouble. Their faith is nearly dead and their works have been found wanting in the sight of God. Works testify to love, or lack of love in the Church, and it is love that testifies to the faith of Christians. Jesus admonishes the church in Sardis: "Remember then what you received and heard; obey it, and repent. If you do not wake up, I will come like a thief, and you will not know at what hour I will come to you" (Revelation 3:3). But to those in Sardis who faithfully follow Christ, he says, "If you conquer, you will be clothed like them in white robes, and I will not blot your name out of the book of life; I will confess your name before my Father and before his angels" (Revelation 3:5).

Philadelphia – The church at Philadelphia is small and at odds with the local Jewish community. Jesus praises them for their faith and works, and promises them victory over their enemies. Jesus tells them, "Because you have kept my word of patient endurance, I will keep you from the hour of trial that is coming on the whole world to test the inhabitants of the earth" (Revelation 3:10). Who are these "inhabitants of the earth?" They are the people who neglect and deny the Word of God. They choose to live in the world and, as a result, "inhabitants of the earth" are mired in the things of earth, numb to the life of the Spirit. They would rather flail around in muddy waters than enjoy the living waters of understanding and wisdom the Holy Spirit offers. But to those who choose to follow Jesus, he promises, "If you conquer, I will make you a pillar in the temple of my God; you will never go out of it. I will write on you the name of my God, and the name of the city of my God, the new Jerusalem that comes down from my God out of heaven, and my own new name" (Revelation 3:12). Christians, who patiently endure to the end, are claimed by God as his own children and are citizens of the Kingdom of Heaven.

Laodicea –The Church at Laodicea is in serious trouble. They are so involved in their worldly undertakings that they are careless about their Christian commitment. Jesus firmly rejects their half-hearted works, which disgust him. He admonishes them, "For you say, 'I am rich, I have prospered, and I need nothing.' You do not realize that you are wretched, pitiable, poor, blind, and naked" (Revelation 3:17). They are self-righteous and proud, relying on themselves, and taking full credit for accumulating their wealth. "Therefore I counsel you to buy from me gold refined by fire so that you may be rich; and white robes to clothe you and to keep the shame of your nakedness from being seen; and salve to anoint your eyes so that you may see" (Revelation 3:18). Jesus begs them to buy gold refined by fire so they will be purified of sin, white robes of victory so they can enter the heavenly wedding feast, and salve for their eyes so they can see the Truth again and cease foolishly chasing after worldly things. He lovingly invites them to the heavenly banquet: "Listen! I am standing at the door, knocking; if you hear my voice and open the door, I will come in to you and eat with you, and you with me. To the one who conquers I will give a place with me on my throne, just as I myself conquered and sat down with my Father on his throne" (Revelation 3:20-21).

Christ asks nothing less of his Church than obedience to his commandments, the holy works that follow from charity, single-minded loyalty, rejection of worldliness, patient endurance in trials, and a whole-hearted practice, proclamation, and defense of the Faith, without equivocation and without heretical additions or subtractions! For our efforts, Jesus promises victory over the world and eternal happiness for all those who persevere to the end. "Let anyone who has an ear listen to what the Spirit is saying to the churches" (Revelation 3:22).

The Seven Seals

Then John, in the spirit, is invited to view the splendor of heaven and the Lord God Almighty seated upon his throne.[75] In a glorious heavenly vision, he sees twenty-four elders and four living creatures surrounding the throne singing, "You are worthy, our Lord and God, to receive glory and honor and power, for you created all things, and by your will they existed and were created" (Revelation 4:11). Jesus Christ appears, described as "…a Lamb standing as if it had been slaughtered, having seven horns and seven eyes, which are the seven spirits of God sent out into all the earth" (Revelation 5:6). The Lamb possesses the fullness of strength and power (the seven horns) and complete knowledge and wisdom (the seven eyes). Christ is the victorious "Lamb of God." He alone is worthy to open the seven seals affixed to the scroll, which he receives from the hand of our Father, and all creatures praise God.[76] The opening of the seals brings about a time of political and natural chaos and suffering caused by humankind's sin. The suffering is allowed by God to soften hearts and bring about conversions.

As the Lamb opens each of the first four seals, a horse and rider is called forth. The first seal reveals a white horse and "... Its rider had a bow; a crown was given him, and he came out conquering and to conquer" (Revelation 6:2). The white horse and rider affirm the ultimate victory of Christ and is a hope to Christians who must endure evil times. The second horse is red; the color of war, which has been, is, and will be, as long sin exists. "... Its rider was permitted to take peace from the earth, so that people would slaughter one another; and he was given a great sword (Revelation 6:4). The third horse is black and its rider carries scales, representing famine, scarceness, and severe inflation that exist because[77] "...the love of many will grow cold..."[78] The opening of the fourth seal reveals a pale green horse. "... Its rider's name was Death, and Hades followed with him; they were given authority over a fourth of the earth, to kill with sword, famine, and pestilence, and by the wild animals of the earth" (Revelation 6:8). Death is the result of sin. The four horsemen are released to render the consequences of sin upon the earth.

The opening of the fifth seal reveals the souls of the martyrs who persevered and died defending the Word of God. They plead with God for justice, but the end has not yet come. They are given white robes and asked to rest and be patient a little longer.[79] These holy ones enjoy eternal glory but the time for God's judgment that will answer their prayers for justice has not yet come. God is still offering humankind his mercy and forgiveness of sins.

Then, a great cataclysm. At the opening of the sixth seal "... there came a great earthquake; the sun became black as sackcloth, the full moon became like blood, and the stars of the sky fell to the earth ..." (Revelation

6:12-13).[80] The heavens and earth are shaken, and all people, rich and poor, powerful and common folk run in terror to created things, caves and mountains, as protection from God's imminent judgment, instead of turning to the Creator, acknowledging their sin, and praying for forgiveness. The angels mark all who are faithful to God with a seal upon their foreheads. The children of Israel who turn to Christ receive God's seal.[81] They belong to God. The uncountable multitude of people from "… every nation, from all tribes and peoples and languages…" (Revelation 7:9), rejoice before the throne of God. "… 'These are they who have come out of the great ordeal; they have washed their robes and made them white in the blood of the Lamb'" (Revelations 7:14). They have conquered sin and are welcomed into the heavenly wedding banquet. Anyone without a white wedding garment will be thrown "… into the outer darkness, where there will be weeping and gnashing of teeth" (Matthew 22:13).

After the opening of the seventh seal, there is silence. The final events will play out now. The prayers of the saints are mixed with incense and rise before God. God answers prayers. An angel throws fire from the heavenly altar down to the earth, and the earth quakes. Seven angels with trumpets are revealed.[82] Each person must choose good or evil, God or Satan, and that choice will define his or her eternal life! Divine justice is at hand. Yet, in his love, God still offers his grace and forgiveness, even if only one soul turns to him.

The Seven Trumpets

As the first four angels blow their trumpets, plagues afflict one third of the earth, an increase from one fourth of the earth affected by disaster when the seals were opened. At the sound of the first two trumpets, fire from heaven burns up a third of the earth, one third of the sea becomes like blood, sea creatures die, and ships are destroyed.[83] At the sound of the third trumpet, one third of the water is polluted and many die.[84] At the sound of the fourth trumpet, one third of the sun, the moon, and the stars are darkened.[85] Disasters follow one after another, but they do not destroy all humankind. Their purpose is the salvation of souls.

"Then I looked, and I heard an eagle crying with a loud voice as it flew in midheaven, 'Woe, woe, woe to the inhabitants of the earth, at the blasts of the other trumpets that the three angels are about to blow!" (Revelations 8:13).

When the eagle cries out the three woes, it is for the "inhabitants of the earth," that he mourns. They are worldly people who suffer greatly during this time because they are defenseless in spiritual warfare. Those who live in the Holy Spirit are not unaffected by the suffering in the world, but they are not afraid. They wear the armor of God. They trust in God's love, as their peaceful, patient endurance attests. "There is no fear in love, but perfect love casts out fear; for fear has to do with punishment, and whoever fears has not reached perfection in love" (1 John 4:18). It is important to sincerely develop your spiritual life and cultivate an intimate relationship with God to be able to remain in God's love and guard against temptations that weaken the soul's resolve. Pray. Keep the Faith. Christ promises, "Because you have kept my word of patient endurance, I will keep you from the hour of trial that is coming on the whole world to test the inhabitants of the earth" (Revelation 3:10).

"And the fifth angel blew his trumpet, and I saw a star that had fallen from heaven to earth, and he was given the key to the shaft of the bottomless pit; he opened the shaft of the bottomless pit, and from the shaft rose smoke like the smoke of a great furnace, and the sun and the air were darkened with the smoke from the shaft" (Revelations 9:1-2). The fallen star, a fallen angel of Satan, opens hell and releases locust-like creatures whose sole purpose is to torment for five months "only those people who do not have the seal of God on their foreheads" (Revelation 9:4). God allows this foretaste of the Satan's cruelty as a warning to the "inhabitants of the earth." When sixth angel blows his trumpet, a great war ensues. The vastness of the army represents how very evil the world has become. One third of humankind is killed.[86] But, despite the horror, the remaining "inhabitants of the earth" continue to worship false gods and refuse to repent of their sins. In their hardness of heart, they reject God's calls to conversion through the suffering that he allows to open their eyes, so that they may repent and save their souls.[87] The first woe ends.

In a short aside, an angel hands John a small open scroll and tells him to eat it. The scroll tastes sweet but sours his stomach. Prophecy is a great gift from God but can contain bitter Truth. John is told, "…You must prophesy again about many peoples and nations and languages and kings."

(Revelation 10:11)

A magnificent angel appears and announces, "… There will be no more delay, but in the days when the seventh angel is to blow his trumpet, the mystery of God will be fulfilled, as he announced to his servants the prophets" (Revelation 10:6-7). John is told, "…Come and measure the temple of God and the altar and those who worship there, but do not measure the court outside the temple; leave that out, for it is given over to the nations, and they will trample over the holy city for forty-two months" (Revelation 11:1-2). For the three and one half years[88] that the holy city is desecrated by idolaters, the Church is protected. Evil is only allowed into the outer courts. For the same length of time, two holy prophets, whose powers are similar to the great prophets of the Old Testament, call the world to repentance and conversion. They are martyred in the streets of Jerusalem, and for three and a half days people refuse to allow them to be buried. The "inhabitants of the earth" celebrate their deaths because the words of prophets made them uncomfortable in their sin. After three and a half days, the prophets are raised from the dead and ascend into heaven, a great sign of the reward awaiting those who persevere to the end. Then an earthquake destroys one-tenth of the city.[89] "… Seven thousand[90] people were killed in the earthquake, and the rest were terrified and gave glory to the God of heaven" (Revelation 11:13). In the great tragedy, hearts are converted and souls turn to God. The second woe is ended and, with the blowing of the next trumpet, the third woe begins.

"Then the seventh angel blew his trumpet, and there were loud voices in heaven saying, 'The kingdom of the world has become the kingdom of our Lord and of his Messiah, and he will reign forever and ever'" (Revelation 11:15). The twenty-four elders sing a beautiful, encouraging canticle announcing that the time for reward and punishment has arrived.[91] All people learn God's justice. The third woe begins.

But first, there is a short recap of salvation history. The Redeemer is born, escapes the devil and is taken up to heaven. Jesus conquered death and the devil when he rose from the dead and ascended into heaven. He redeemed the world, freeing humankind from Satan's grasp. The woman, the Church that bears Christ to the world, is protected by God's grace from Satan's wrath. Frustrated that he cannot destroy the Church, Satan attacks the Church's children, those who keep the Word of God[92] Then, Satan, the dragon, makes a blasphemous beast come out of the sea. This sea beast has seemingly miraculous power and exercises its power over all of the people on earth. A second beast comes out of the earth, a trio of Evil, mocking the Holy Trinity. The earth beast exercises the full evil authority of the sea beast, working wonders that persuade the inhabitants of the earth to worship the sea beast. All must accept his mark, the number

666, on their hands or foreheads, mocking the seal God placed upon his children's foreheads. The "inhabitants of the earth" worship the sea beast, and God's children suffer because of sin in the world. Through trickery and deception, Satan consolidates worldwide political power and controls all of the nations. The world's economic systems, setting interest rates on money that can be borrowed, world trade, all markets, even individual sales and purchases of food, homes, clothing, health care, and other necessities, are regulated by a one-world economic system. All trade is governed by this evil system and the mark of the Beast.[93]

> *Revelation is given to John on an intensely spiritual level. He experiences the secrets God shares with him for the benefit of humankind on a much greater than human level, for with each revelation from God comes extraordinary spiritual understanding. Much symbolism is used and Revelation must be read with spiritual insight not literally.*

The dragon's war is not like other wars. The battle lines are drawn within hearts and souls. The weapons are prayer and God's grace on one side, and Satan's terror and deception on the other. Satan empowers his beasts and God allows a time of great evil in the world so that those who are on their way to hell will see beforehand the horror they are choosing and, perhaps, be converted. There are only two sides: those who worship God in Spirit and in Truth and are sealed by God, and those who worship the beast, by either choice or default, and are sealed by his mark. Those who are sealed by God are sustained by grace. God is with them in a way unknown since the time of the apostles.

We again see the joy-filled faithful singing before the throne of God. "...No one could learn that song except the one hundred forty-four thousand who have been redeemed from the earth (Revelation 14:3). One hundred and forty-four thousand (12 x 12 x 1,000) represents all of the followers of Christ, including all converted Jews and all followers of Jesus' apostles. The description, "It is these who have not defiled themselves with women, for they are virgins; ..." (Revelation 14:4) does not mean that only one hundred and forty-four thousand virgin males will go to heaven as some cults would have us believe. The 144,000 "redeemed from the earth" are all faithful followers of Christ. These verses can be understood in light of inspired scripture. As we have already seen, scripture compares idolatry to fornication.[94] Paul wrote to the church in Corinth: "I feel a divine jealousy for you, for I promised you in marriage to one husband, to present you as a chaste virgin to Christ. But I am afraid that as the serpent deceived Eve by its cunning, your thoughts will be led astray from a pure and sincere devotion to Christ" (2 Corinthians 11:2-3). The 144,000 are the entire Church, the holy Bride of Christ, those who practice "a pure and sincere devotion to Christ."

After this heavenly interlude, three angels appear. The first cries out, "...Fear God and give him glory, for the hour of his judgment has come; and worship him who made heaven and earth, the seas and the springs of water" (Revelation 14:7). The second angel announces, "... 'Fallen, fallen is Babylon the great! She has made all nations drink of the wine of the wrath of her fornication'" (Revelation 14:8). "Inhabitants of the earth" who place their faith in Babylon, the city that worships false gods and trusts in its own power and glory, will suffer her punishment. The third angel very explicitly describes the hell that awaits those who follow the beast.[95]

"Here is a call for the endurance of the saints, those who keep the commandments of God and hold fast to the faith of Jesus" (Revelation 14:12). The faithful must hold on a little longer. The first Christians did not abandon ship when they experienced persecution for the first three centuries of the Church's existence. On the contrary, their patient endurance drew many people to Christ. Christians in the last days are called to follow their example.

"He put before them another parable: 'The kingdom of heaven may be compared to someone who sowed good seed in his field; but while everybody was asleep, an enemy came and sowed weeds among the wheat, and then went away. So when the plants came up and bore grain, then the weeds appeared as well. And the slaves of the householder came and said to him, 'Master, did you not sow good seed in your field? Where, then, did these weeds come from?' 'He answered, 'An enemy has done this.' The slaves said to him, 'Then do you want us to go and gather them?' But he replied, 'No; for in gathering the weeds you would uproot the wheat along with them. Let both of them grow together until the harvest; and at harvest time I will tell the reapers, Collect the weeds first and bind them into bundles to be burned, but gather the wheat into my barn'" (Matthew 13:24-30). It is harvest time. Jesus, the just judge, swings the sickle himself and harvests the earth, and gathers the faithful to himself.[96] The wicked, who worship the beast, are gathered and experience the wrath of God.[97] Those, who kept their faith are victorious and sing of God's mercy and justice: "…Just and true are your ways, King of the nations! Lord, who will not fear and glorify your name?" (Revelation 15:3-4). This interlude is a promise of justice for those who patiently endure. "Then I saw another portent in heaven, great and amazing: seven angels with seven plagues, which are the last, for with them the wrath of God is ended" (Revelation 15:1).

The Seven Bowls

The seven angels are robed in white with gold sashes. Each angel carries a bowl of God's wrath, plagues reminiscent of the plagues inflicted upon the pagan Egyptians in the time of Moses. The first angel's bowl causes painful sores on those who wear the mark of the beast. The second angel's bowl causes the sea to turn to blood and all of the fish die. The third angel's bowl causes all fresh water to turn to blood and the angel says "…'You are just, O Holy One, who are and who were, for you have judged these things; because they shed the blood of saints and prophets, you have given them blood to drink. It is what they deserve!'" (Revelation 16:5-6). The fourth angel's bowl causes the heat from the sun to intensify and, "they were scorched by the fierce heat, but they cursed the name of God, who had authority over these plagues, and they did not repent and give him glory" (Revelation 16:9).[98]

The fifth bowl of God's wrath is directed at the throne of the beast, "… and its kingdom was plunged into darkness" (Revelation 16:10). Yet, those who carry the mark of the Beast, facing the overwhelming power of God's wrath, stubbornly continue to choose hell.[99] The sixth angel's bowl is poured out and the world is stirred up for war. Demonic frog-like spirits leap from the mouths of the Evil Trio and are sent "to the kings of the whole world, to assemble them for battle on the great day of God the Almighty" (Revelation 16:14). They gather at Armageddon.

"See, I am coming like a thief! Blessed is the one who stays awake and is clothed, not going about naked and exposed to shame" (Revelation 16:15). Those who listen are admonished to remain vigilant against temptation and remain in God, clothed in grace and good works. Those who continue to worship the beast have nothing to show for their lives but their shameful works, on which they will be judged.

The seventh angel pours out his bowl into the air. Violent storms and earthquakes result, as have never been seen before; one hundred pound hailstones drop on people. Islands and mountains disappear and great cities fall. Still, the "inhabitants of the earth" curse God.[100]

The End of Babylon

John is invited to witness the judgment of Babylon. She is a whore who sits upon a blasphemous beast,[101] "with whom the kings of the earth have committed fornication, and with the wine of whose fornication the inhabitants of the earth have become drunk" (Revelation 17:2). By their idolatry, the inhabitants of the earth have sinned against God. Babylon is self-indulgent and arrogant. Trusting in her financial prosperity, she lures the nations by her cult of luxury and consumerism. She exports her sinful ideology to all nations, and she murders Christians. [102] She revels in her evil deeds, but God has decreed that her time has come to an end. An angel tells John that the kings of the earth will ally themselves with the blasphemous beast against Babylon and destroy her, "For God has put it into their hearts to carry out his purpose by agreeing to give their kingdom to the beast, until the words of God will be fulfilled" (Revelation 17:17). Babylon's own allies destroy her and thus God's judgment is fulfilled. The blasphemous beast and the kings of the earth "…will make war on the Lamb, and the Lamb will conquer them, for he is Lord of lords and King of kings, and those with him are called and chosen and faithful" (Revelation 17:14).

What of God's people who live in Babylon? "Then I heard another voice from heaven saying, 'Come out of her, my people, so that you do not partake in her sins, and so that you do not share in her plagues" (Revelation 18:4). God protects them from the spiritual and physical dangers present in Babylon. Jesus said, "I am the good shepherd. I know my own and my own know me" (John 10:14). By gifts of God's grace, the faithful know and hear God in a deeply interior life of the Spirit, and God guides his people to safety. Evil is great all over the world and the faithful endure the pain of watching the "inhabitants of the earth," who seem very powerful, blaspheme God. The faithful must be vigilant to avoid becoming lost in the evil and confusion. "Be on guard so that your hearts are not weighed down with dissipation and drunkenness and the worries of this life, and that day does not catch you unexpectedly, like a trap. For it will come upon all who live on the face of the whole earth. Be alert at all times, praying that you may have the strength to escape all these things that will take place, and to stand before the Son of Man" (Luke 21:34-36). But the faithful also have the comfort of recognizing God's grace in action as they turn to prayer and each other for help and comfort, like Christians in the early days of the Church.

Jesus keeps his promise to his Apostles that they would judge with him. "Then I saw thrones, and those seated on them were given authority to judge..." (Revelation 20:4).

An angel proclaims a lament over Babylon, "...It has become a dwelling place of demons..." (Revelation 18:2). Arrogant Babylon falls suddenly and is mourned by the shocked "inhabitants of the earth" whom she had made wealthy. Kings, merchants, and seafarers mourn the loss of the source of their prosperity, and the luxuries they had become accustomed to "...For in one hour she has been laid waste. Rejoice over her, O heaven, you saints and apostles and prophets! For God has given judgment for you against her" (Revelation 18:19-20). The saints' prayers for justice are answered and there is rejoicing in heaven. "After this I heard what seemed to be the loud voice of a great multitude in heaven, saying, 'Hallelujah! Salvation and glory and power to our God, for his judgments are true and just; he has judged the great whore who corrupted the earth with her fornication, and he has avenged on her the blood of his servants.'" (Revelation 19:1-2)

The Justice of God

"Then I saw heaven opened, and there was a white horse! Its rider is called Faithful and True, and in righteousness he judges and makes war" (Revelation 19:11). He is Christ the Lord, and his heavenly white-robed cavalry follows him. He rules with absolute authority and dispenses justice. The armies of the kings of the earth ally themselves with the beast and assemble at Armageddon for battle.[103] The sharp sword from the mouth of Christ destroys his enemies, in testimony to the power of the Word of God. Before the battle begins, an angel calls birds to feast on the slain bodies of the beast's armies saying, "…Come, gather for the great supper of God…" (Revelation 19:17) This is the doom of those who follow the beast. This supper contrasts sharply with the reward given to the holy ones. They are invited to the "…the marriage supper of the Lamb…" (Revelation 19:9). They are filled with joy and no longer have any needs or desires, for all good things belong to them. The beast from the earth and the sea beast (a.k.a. the false prophet) are "…thrown alive into the lake of fire that burns with sulfur" (Revelation 19:20). Satan is chained in hell for a symbolic one thousand years, a long time, but not forever, yet.[104]

Augustine of Hippo taught that Satan's power has been chained up since Christ's Resurrection, that is, limited by the salvation and forgiveness of sins Christ gained for us, and Christ reigns fully in his Church (Faculty of Theology of the University of Navarre). Now, the Gates of Heaven are open to those who die and rise in Christ through baptism,[105] and those who die in Christ reign with him. Did Jesus not tell the repentant thief who hung crucified beside him, "… 'today you will be with me in Paradise?'" (Luke 23:43). "Blessed and holy are those who share in the first resurrection. Over these the second death has no power, but they will be priests of God and of Christ and they will reign with him a thousand years" (Revelation 20:6). The first resurrection is the admittance of baptized holy souls into heaven after they suffer physical death. The second resurrection will restore the souls of both the good and the evil to their bodies. The un-baptized, "The rest of the dead did not come to life until the thousand years were ended" (Revelation 20:5). What of the "rest of the dead?" At the Final Judgment, Christ will judge them based upon their deeds. The second death is God's justice rendered at the Final Judgment of the wicked who will join Satan in the lake of fire for all eternity.[106]

Satan was chained up at Christ's Resurrection. Since then, Christians have enjoyed a time of Christ's grace and peace, but the era of peace appears to be ending. Satan has been angrily struggling against his chains, but he cannot free himself. The angel "…threw him into the pit, and locked and sealed it over him…" (Revelation 20:3). Satan needs an "outside man" to break him out. Just who is this "outside man" helping Satan? Every person who rejects God and his commandments and allows himself to be influenced by Satan, loosens Satan's chains. The populace is demanding Satan's freedom, opening the seal to the pit and unchaining him, for they have chosen him as their leader.

"When the thousand years are ended, Satan will be released from his prison and will come out to deceive the nations at the four corners of the earth, Gog and Magog, in order to gather them for battle; they are as numerous as the sands of the sea" (Revelation 20:7-8) Satan is angrier, cleverer, and more hateful than ever. He knows his end is near and he wants to steal as many souls away from God as possible. He wants every human soul to follow him into the lake of fire and sulfur for all eternity. He stirs up war and chaos and many follow him. Satan is released because the populace demands it! "They marched up over the breadth of the earth and surrounded the camp of the saints and the beloved city. And fire came down from heaven and consumed them. And the devil who had deceived them was thrown into the lake of fire and sulfur, where the beast and the false prophet were, and they will be tormented day and night forever and ever"

(Revelation 20:9-10). The armies that attack "the beloved city" in the final battle are defeated by God's own hand and Satan is finished.

Who are Gog and Magog?

Their actual identities are unclear. In chapters 38 and 39, Ezekiel prophesies that Gog, a land from the north, and Magog will ally themselves with Persia (Iran), Ethiopia, Put (Libya), Gomer, and armies from the remotest part of the north to attack Israel. God him-self defeats the great army and Israel has peace. Read Ezekiel 38 and 39 for more insight.

"Then they will see 'the Son of Man coming in a cloud' with power and great glory. Now when these things begin to take place, stand up and raise your heads, because your redemption is drawing near" (Luke 21: 27-2).

The human being consists of physical body and a spiritual soul that makes us heirs to eternal life. The spiritual soul makes us different from animals that have no free will and cannot make choices. They act by instinct and are not responsible for their actions. By contrast, angels in heaven are entirely spiritual beings with free wills. They have no physical bodies. Because of our dual nature, our souls must be reunited with our natural bodies for us to be complete, therefore, at the Final Judgment all souls will be rejoined with their bodies. "And the sea gave up the dead that were in it, Death and Hades gave up the dead that were in them, and all were judged according to what they had done" (Revelation 20:13). Those whose names are written in the book of life enjoy the Kingdom of God, "...and I will be their God and they will be my children. But as for the cowardly, the faithless, the polluted, the murderers, the fornicators, the sorcerers, the idolaters, and all liars, their place will be in the lake that burns with fire and sulfur, which is the second death" (Revelation 21:7-8).

There are two comings of Christ. He was born to redeem us, and he will come a second time, at the Last Judgment. His people rejoice that Christ's promises are coming to fulfillment.

The Bride of Christ, the gloriously beautiful holy city Jerusalem, made of a clear pure gold, is revealed. Its twelve foundations, upon which are written the names of the twelve apostles, are adorned with precious gems, and upon its twelve pearl gates are written the names of the twelve tribes of Israel. Such is the beauty and glory of the holy souls who dwell securely within the city. Never again will they know fear, sorrow, hunger, or thirst. God will dwell with his beloved people and supply all their needs. In Jerusalem, all will be fulfilled, and people will glorify God, and live in his glory. There will be true peace on a new earth.

Thanks and praise to God for his loving kindness. His Will be done!

END NOTES

[1]   Acts:8:9-24

[2]   Acts 18:2-3 – "…Paul went to see them, and, because he was of the same trade, he stayed with them, and they worked together – by trade they were tentmakers." 1 Thessalonians 2:9 – "You remember our labor and toil, brother and sisters; we worked night and day, so that we might not burden any of you while we proclaimed to you the gospel of God."

[3]   See John 4:7-30. It was considered inappropriate for a man to speak to a woman alone, and even more inappropriate to speak to a Samaritan woman, and most inappropriate accept a drink from her. The Jews did not associate with the Samaritans whom they regarded as second-class citizens.

[4]   See Mark 8:1-9, Matthew 14:15-21 and 15:32-38

[5]   See Matthew 14:1-14

[6]   Added for clarity

[7]   See Galatians 1 and 2

[8]   Green Stamps were given to customers as a reward for making purchases, for example, ten stamps for each dollar spent. The stamps were then pasted in books and each book was "redeemed" in a store called a Redemption Center where all merchandise was priced in numbers of books. This method of rewarding customers fell out of favor in the 1970's.

[9]   Genesis 5:1

[10]   Genesis 2:16

11   Genesis 3:12-13

12   Read Genesis Chapter 3

13   Revelations 12:7-9

14   God-given extraordinary gifts of grace that protected Adam and Eve from the weaknesses of human nature i.e. freedom from illness and death.

15   Genesis 1:1 and John 1:1

16   See 2 Timothy 4:3-4

17   Read Genesis Chapters 6, 7 and 8.

18   Read Genesis 11:27 - 25:10 for the story of Abraham's personal relationship with God.

19   See Leviticus 18:21 and 20:1-5. The Lord clearly forbids the Canaanite practice of sacrificing children to the pagan god Molech. In Ezekiel 20:21-31,the sacrifice of the first born child is seen as punishment of the Israelites for abusing God's Law; God required them to redeem their first born sons by offering a lamb or dove in the children's places. Appalled, God leaves them to their free-will choice of abandoning him in favor of following pagan rituals that required the murder of their children.

20   Read Genesis 22:1-19.

21   Genesis 35:1-15

22   Read Genesis: 37 and 39-50 for the full story.

23   Genesis 45:16-20

24   See Exodus chapters 28, 29 and 30 for the details.

25   See Leviticus for God's instructions to the Israelites regarding worship.

26   Luke 2:25-35

[27] Luke 2:36-38

[28] Exodus 3:14

[29] Luke 20:45-47, John 8:12-53, Mark 7:1-12 for example

[30] See Genesis 4: 8-17 for the rest of the story.

[31] Italics that show Jesus in prayer are added for emphasis in the first section of "Lord, Teach Us to Pray."

[32] (the gifts) and (the gifts of God's Spirit) added for clarity

[33] Revelation 3:10

[34] John 19:25

[35] See Mark 16:2-6, Acts 2:1, Acts 20:7

[36] See Mark 3:1-6 and John 5:1-16

[37] See Mark 3:6 and Matthew 12:9-14

[38] See Genesis 2:18-23

[39] See Luke 2:51

[40] Also see Sirach (Ecclesiasticus) 3:1-16

[41] See Leviticus 18:21

[42] Emphasis is from the original document.

[43] Names are changed.

[44] See the summer, 2011 case of M, a woman whose family sued in the English Court of Protection to have artificial hydration and nutrition discontinued. The family contended that M would not have wanted to live in a dependent state. The Judge ruled against the removal of food and water.

See the case of 2005 case of Terri Schiavo in Florida, USA, whose husband, Michael Schiavo, won a court ruling to have artificial hydration and nutrition withheld from his wife over the objection of her parents who were willing to take guardianship of her.

45   See John 8:1-11

46   See Matthew 12: 34-35

47   See   http://nypost.com/2014/08/03/sharpton-demands-accountability-but-still-owes-millions-in-back-taxes/

48   See 1 John 2:3-6

49   See Philippians 3:7-11

50   Matthew 4:18-22, Mark 2:14 for example

51   John 21:4-14

52   See John 12:1-8.

53   Hymenaeus and Philetus claimed that the resurrection of the body that Jesus promised us when he returned had already happened at baptism when a person was raised from their sinful life thus causing confusing. This is heresy

54   See the details in Exodus chapters 26-31 and 36-40.

55   See 1 Timothy 4:14, 1 Timothy 5:22

56   4F is a military service classification in the United States of America. 4F means an individual is exempt from military service because of physical or mental impairment.

57   From a poem by Martin Niemoller, a Protestant defender of the faith, who spent seven years in a Nazi prison.

58   Rumors spread the Christians were cannibals because they ate the body of Christ and drank his blood. Pagans could not understand the Last Supper

meal in Christian celebrations, the breaking of the bread at the Eucharistic Feast.

59   1 Corinthians 12:27 for example

60   Parenthesis (Christ) added for clarity

61   See Acts 13:2 for example

62   See Matthew 2:1-18

63   See Acts 9:23-25 and 29-30,

64   When Jesus was presented in the Temple in Jerusalem, Simeon said to Mary, Jesus mother, "…This child is destined for the falling and rising of many in Israel, and to be a sign that will be opposed so that the inner thoughts of many will be revealed…"(Luke 2:34-35).

65   (God) inserted for clarity

66   See John19:19-22. Pontius Pilate was adamant that the inscription be worded exactly as quoted in spite of the protestations of the chief priests.

67   (Jesus) inserted for clarity

68   Matthew 24:8

69   Revelation 21:1

70   See Revelation 1:11

71   See Revelation 2:10

72   See Revelation 20:14-15

73   Jezebel, the wife of Ahab, King of Israel, promoted the worship of Baal and murdered the prophets of God.. Through the prophet Elijah, God decrees his judgment against her. See 1 Kings 21. She meets with a most unpleasant end. See 2 Kings 9.

74   "Adultery" and "fornication" were words used in the Old Testament to describe unfaithfulness to God. See Ezekiel 23 for example.

75   Revelation 4:1-7

76   See Revelation chapter 5

77   Revelation 6:5-6

78   See Matthew 24:12

79   See Revelations 6:9-11

80   Also see Joel 2:30-32

81   See Revelation 7:1-8

82   See Revelations 8:1-5

83   See Revelations 8:7-9

84   See Revelations 8:10-11

85   See Revelation 8:12

86   See Revelation 9:13-19

87   See Revelation 9:20-21

88   Three and one half years or forty-two months or one thousand two hundred and sixty days all designate one half of the three and one half represent a limited time.

89   See Revelation 11:3 – 11:13

90   Seven represents all the classes of people from rich to poor and one thousand symbolizes a very large but not unlimited number.

91   See Revelation 11:15-18

92   See Revelation 12:1-6 and 12:13-17

93   See Revelation 12:17 – 13:18

94   See Ezekiel 23 and Hosea 5:3-7 for examples

95   See Revelation 14: 9-11

96   See Revelation 14:14-16

97   See Revelation 14:17-20

98   See Revelation 16:1-9

99   See Revelation 16:10-11

100   See Revelation 16: 12-21

101   The beast is called the one who "…was and is not and is to come," (Revelation 17:8) mocking Christ's title as the one "…who is, who was and who is to come" (Revelation 1:8).

102   There are other interpretations of Revelation 17 and 18, but most agree that the imagery depicts the fall of Rome, the city that killed the saints.

103   Revelation 16:16

104   See Revelation 19:11-20:3

105   See Romans 6:4

106   See Revelation 20:11-15

BIBLIOGRAPHY

Aquilina, Mike. "The Fathers of the Church, An Introduction to the First Christian Teachers." Huntington: Our Sunday Visitor, 2006. 42-44. Print.

Blair, Leonard. "ISIS Torches 1,800-Year-Old Church in Mosul, Priest Says City is 'Now Empty of Christians.'" 21 July 2014. *The Christian Post.* Web Page. 16 November 2015. <http://www.christianpost.com/news/isis-torches-1800-year-old-church-in-mosul-priest-says-city-is-now-empty-of-christians-123632/>.

Bush, George W. "Executive Order 13435 Expanding Approved Stem Cell Lines in Ethically Responsible Ways." 20 June 2007. *United States Government Printing Office.* Web site. 13 August 2015. <http://gpo.gov/fdsys/pkg/FR-2007-06-22/pdf/07-3112.pdf>.

California Institute for Regenerative Medicine. *Myths and Misconceptions about Stem Cell Research.* January 2015. Internet. 10 August 2015. <https://www.cirm.ca.gov/patients/myths-and-misconceptions-about-stem-cell-research >.

Chapman, John. "Nestorius and Nestorianism." *The Catholic Encyclopedia.* Vol. 10. New York: Robert Appleton Company, 1911, n.d. 21 Sept 2013. <http://www.newadvent.org/cathen/10755a.htm>.

Clark, Kelly James. "The Most Persecuted Religion in the World." *The World Post* 04 01 2013: na. 19 02 2014. <http://www.huffingtonpost.com/kelly-james-clark/christianity-most-persecuted-religion_b_...>.

Craine, Patrick. "DC Archdiocese Priest-blogger: America is One Step Away From Persecution." 29 November 2012. *Life Site News.* Web site. 16 November 2015. <https://www.lifesitenews.com/all/date/2012/12/04>.

"David Koresh." 11 August 2014. *Wikipedia, The Free Encyclopedia.* Retrieved 17:05, 23 August 2014. <http://en.wikipedia.org/w/index.php?title=David_Koresh&oldid=620807205>.

Faculty of Theology of the University of Navarre. *The Navarre Bible, Book of Revelation, Text and Commentaries.* Ed. Brian Mccarthy, Thomas McGoven James Gavigan. Dublin: Four Courts Press, 2001. Book.

Harkness, Kelsey. "They Lost Their Bakery, Now Face Bankruptcy: Government's 'Discrimination' Fine Brings Baker to Tears." 29 September 2014. *The Daily Signal.* Web site. 16 November 2015. <http://dailysignal.com/2014/09/29/lost-bakery-now-face-bankruptcy-governments-discrimination-fine-brings-oregon-baker-tears>.

Health Day. "States Now Fund Most Embryonic Stem Cell Research in U.S." 14 December 2010. *U.S. News and World Report.* Web page. 21 August 2015.

History.com Staff. "Dred Scott Case." 2009. *History.com.* A+E Networks. Web page. 11 August 2015. <http://www.history.com/topics/black-history/dred-scott-case>.

"Jim Jones." 18 August 2014. *Wikipedia, The Free Encyclopedia.* Retrieved 16:42, 23 August 2014. <http://en.wikipedia.org/w/index.php?title=Jim_Jones&oldid=621734005>.

Leclercq, Henri. "The First Council of Nicea." *The Catholic Encyclopedia.* Vol. 11. New York: Robert Appleton Company, 1911. 1 July 2015. <http://www.newadvent.org/cathen/11044a.htm>.

Matthews, D. Wayne. *Long-term Effects of Divorce on Children.* Raleigh: North Carolina Cooperative Extension Service, 1998. Print. 9 June 2015. <http://www.ces.ncsu.edu/depts/fcs/pdfs/fcs482.pdf>.

Montoya, Orlando. "Agency: Prayer Ban a Misunderstanding." 10 May 2010. *GPB News.* Web. 16 November 2015. <http://www.gpb.org/news/2010/05/10/agency-prayer-ban-a-misunderstanding >.

National Institutes of Health. "Human Embryonic Stem Cell Policy Under Former President Bush (Aug. 9, 2001 - Mar. 9, 2009) In Stem Cell Information." 10 March 2009. *National Institutes of Health, U.S. Department of Health and Human Services.* Web . 13 August 2015. <http://stemcells.nih.gov/policy/pages/2001policy.aspx>.

New Health Guide. "When Does A Baby Have A Heartbeat?" 19 August 2015. *New Health Guide.* Web Page. 19 August 2015. <http://www.newhealthguide.org/When-Does-A-Baby-Have-A-Heartbeat.htm>.

Obama, Barak. "Removing Barriers to Responsible Scientific Research Involving Human Stem Cells." 9 March 2009. *United States Government Printing Office.* Web page. 13 August 2015. <http://www.gpo.gov/fdsys/pkg/FR-2009-03-11/pdf/E9-5441.pdf>.

"Oxford Living Dictionaries." January 2014. *Freedom of conscience.* 5 March 2014. <https://en.oxforddictionaries.com/definition/us/freedom_of_conscience>.

Raynard S. Kingston, M.D., Ph.D. "Stem Cell Information." 12 January 2011. *U.S. Department of Health and Human Services.* Web site. 21 August 2015. <http://stemcells.nih.gov/policy/Pages/2009guidelines.aspx>.

Shirer, William L. *The Rise and Fall of the Third Reich, A History of Nazi Germany.* New York: Rosetta Books, LLC, 2011. E-book.

"Shoko Asahara." 29 July 2014. *Wikipedia, The Free Encyclopedia.* Retrieved 16:44, 24 August 2014. <http://en.wikipedia.org/w/index.php?title=Shoko_Asahara&oldid=619035492>.

The Faculty of Theology of the University of Navarre, John. *The Navarre Bible, The Book of Revelation, Text and Commentaries.* Ed. Brian McCarthy, Thomas McGovern James Gavigan. Trans. Michael Adams. Dublin: Four Courts Press, 2001. Print.

William Allan Neilson, Ph.D., LL.D. ,L.H.D., Litt.D., Thomas A. Knott, Ph.D., Paul W. Carhart, ed. *Webster's New International Dictionary of the English Language, Second Edition, Unabridged.* Springfield: G. & C. Merriam Company, 1944. Print.